Be a Millionaire Shopkeeper

*How Your Independent Shop Can
Compete with the Big Guys*

Joanna Bradshaw

iUniverse LLC
Bloomington

Be a Millionaire Shopkeeper
How Your Independent Shop Can Compete with the Big Guys

iUniverse books may be ordered through booksellers or by contacting:

iUniverse
1663 Liberty Drive
Bloomington, IN 47403
www.iuniverse.com
1-800-Authors (1-800-288-4677)

ISBN: 978-1-4759-4140-1 (sc)
ISBN: 978-1-4759-4139-5 (hc)
ISBN: 978-1-4759-4138-8 (e)

Library of Congress Control Number: 2012913774

Printed in the United States of America

iUniverse rev. date: 8/2/2013

Contents

Acknowledgments

I want to thank four very special, talented people who contributed greatly to *Be a Millionaire Shopkeeper,* all of whom I have worked with in the past.

First I must thank Tony Damiano, who was my inspiration for writing this book. Tony began his career as a visual manager for Pottery Barn and became visual director and store planner for the most fashionable home furnishings specialty chains, such as Terrence Conran's very innovative European chain, Conran's Habitat. In 2000 Tony opened Mango Jam, an upscale gift shop in Ridgewood, New Jersey, which has been voted as the best gift shop in Bergen County several times. Very civic-minded, he has served two terms as president of Ridgewood's chamber of commerce before founding the Ridgewood Guild, a business alliance dedicated to "creating a better Ridgewood."

Sharon Adler is largely responsible for the major segment in chapter 7 on trends, how to find them, and how to use them, for which I certainly do want to thank her. She launched her retailing career as a trainee at Abraham and Straus (A&S), where she subsequently held a number of the most creative buyerships (i.e., the Gift Shop) before becoming a global scout, product development merchandiser, and trend and color forecaster for the leading importer to department and specialty stores from the Orient. She is an acknowledged expert in seasonal product development—Christmas and others—and traveled all over the world for the most significant players in this arena before starting her own consulting business in foreign sourcing and product development.

Next I would like to thank Michael Aaronson for his contribution as financial consultant. Michael began his retailing career as an auditor in the Internal Audit Department of Federated's A&S, where he rose to vice president of finance. He went on to assume senior roles in virtually every area of the business—finance, operations, and merchandising. Leading the acquisition team for Sam Goody, he later was the company's chief operating officer before becoming business head of Bergdorf Goodman's merchandising division. After being president of the Rag Shop, a chain of craft and fabric specialty stores, Michael became an entrepreneur and opened a very successful dry-cleaning and valet service serving high-end hotels and businesses. Today he also serves as president of his condo's board.

Finally, I would like to thank my twin brother, Gregory Bradshaw, for his advertising/marketing input. Greg started his career as a product manager for Borden and has spent a full career in marketing management. His specialty is new products commercialization, but he has an unusual background of having worked in an extraordinarily broad range of fields and product categories—from heavy industrial commodities to major packaged goods brands to retail store brand building. He is founder and president of The Marketing House, now in its twenty-sixth year, from which he lectures professionally on classical marketing techniques.

I am sure you will join me in being appreciative of their input as you read *Be a Millionaire Shopkeeper.*

INTRODUCTION

Why Read This Book?

You are probably either an independent retailer or are thinking about becoming one. You are, or will be, joining the ranks of one of the oldest and largest business segments.

According to the 2007 US Economic Census, which is done every five years, and reported by Stacy Mitchell in "What New Census Data Show about the State of Independent Retail," independent retailers (defined as having fewer than ten employees) account for 28 percent of all consumer retail sales (down from 31 percent in 2002), with "approximately 60,000 grocery and specialty food stores, 38,000 clothing shops, 19,000 florists, 18,000 pharmacies, 18,000 furniture stores, 17,000 sporting goods retailers, 12,000 hardware stores, 12,000 nurseries and garden centers, 7,400 appliance stores and 2,700 general bookstores."[1]

Much is being written today about the independent retailer's fight for survival, but the fact is that there have always been new and evolving threats, as there are in any business. In the late 1800s

---

1   Stacy Mitchell, "What New Census Data Show about the State of Independent Retail," December 16, 2010, *Institute for Local Self Reliance*, http//www.ilsr.org/retail.news/what-new-census-data-show-about-state-independent-Retail.html/ (accessed May 6, 2011).

the first department stores started vying for the retail business; then the first chain stores came; and then the giant discounters like Walmart arrived. Next were catalog retailers, and now we have the Internet.

So, while the independents' overall market share is eroding with the advent of these newer types of retailers, independents are still a vital segment of American retail business. Indeed, some categories, such as bakeries and greengrocers, are even growing with the increasing desire to shop at neighborhood stores, Mitchell reports.

Not only do independent retailers account for an awesome amount of business, but there is little doubt that there is still a lot of money to be made as an independent retailer. And don't forget, most of the larger retail operations (even Walmart) were founded by independent retailers who started as owners of single stores!

No doubt about it, though, retailing in any venue has become tougher. The independent retailer has both advantages and disadvantages over the big guys (which I will discuss at length later). The independent, for example, is more agile and can react much more quickly than the larger chains. However, usually untrained as a merchant, the owner often has to rely on instinct, and learns by trial and error. Some believe that today this is one of the independent retailers' greatest weaknesses.

I have been an independent and am also a seasoned, well-trained retailer who has been a significant player in the legendary turnarounds of four retailers: Bloomingdale's, Macy's, Simmons, and Abraham & Straus. I cofounded a 120,000-square-foot category-killer lifestyle chain, and served as senior merchant and president of two upscale specialty store chains, Conran's Habitat and Workbench.

During my career I have learned a great deal about merchandising—sometimes through training, often by trial and error—but I have found over the years that many things worked no matter what type of retail operation I found myself in. The purpose of this book is to share with you what I have learned, to hopefully make you better able to compete with the big guys, as well as with other independents, and perhaps help speed you on your way to making a million … or maybe your next one!

CHAPTER I

Retailing Today

Before opening my retail consulting business, I was a retailer for over forty years. During that time, I learned a great deal about retailing, having experienced the best in all venues—department stores, specialty stores, outlets, big-box retailers, wholesale manufacturers, import marketers, start-ups, turnarounds, and liquidations.

I also loved every minute of it. You may call me a masochist, but the thrill, excitement, and newness of every day always kept me supercharged. As I have often said, for over forty years, I was paid, and handsomely too, to go shopping around the world. What woman could ask for more?

With all that excitement comes change, which many have called the essence of retailing. Over the years I have witnessed a lot of change, but with the present economic climate, the environment is vastly more competitive—and extremely difficult—for the retailer. *Indeed, while there has probably never been a more challenging time for any retailer, especially for the independent, there is still money to be made and success to be had!*

Today we have the following factors:

A Weak Economy

The unemployment rate, the housing slowdown, the credit crunch, the financial meltdown, and fear itself have all severely impacted retail sales. So many people have lost their jobs, had their incomes severely curtailed, or watched their retirement nest eggs dwindle, while the more cautious pundits are still voicing doom and gloom, scaring everyone even more and making them think twice before making any purchase that is not absolutely necessary. Right now the economy is perhaps the most important factor to be confronted and endured, but as they say, this too shall pass. Even as our economy improves, though, it will always be a major factor to be reckoned with—either positively or negatively.

Industry Consolidation

The big are getting bigger and can demand more of everything from qualified workers to enormous concessions from wholesalers. As the big guys expand, they put even more pressure on the independent retailer. The most obvious case in point is the main department stores that have been absorbed by the Macy Corporation and the retailers they had absorbed previously:

Abraham & Straus
Bamberger's
The Bon Marché
Bullock's
Burdines
The Broadway
Davison's
Dayton's
The Denver Dry Goods Company
The Emporium
Famous-Barr
Filene's

Foley's
G. Fox
Frederick & Nelson
Goldwater's
Goldsmith's
Halle Brothers
Hecht's
Hudson's
I. Magnin
The Jones Store
Jordan Marsh
Kaufmann's
Lasalle & Koch
Lazarus
Liberty House
L. S. Ayers
Maas Brothers
Marshall Field's
Meier & Frank
Rich's
Rike-Kumler
J. W. Robinson's
Sanger-Harris
Shillito's
Stern's
Strawbridge & Clothier
Thalhimers
Wanamaker's
Weinstock's
Woodward & Lothrop

Overstoring and Overlapping

There are too many stores to survive, and many of the biggest have already bitten the dust. While you can find the names of hundreds of defunct retailers on the web, the following list identifies just a few of some very significant retailers in every category that no longer exist:

Alexander's
B. Altman & Company
Bonwit Teller
Bradlees
Caldor
Channel Home Centers
Circuit City
Crazy Eddie
E. J. Korvette
Eckerd
Gimbels
Grand Union
Hills Supermarkets
J. J. Newberry
Kinney Shoes
Lechters Housewares
Levitz Furniture
Lechmere
Linens 'n Things
Mervyn's
Montgomery Ward
Rickel
Robert Hall
Seaman's
Service Merchandise
Two Guys
W. T. Grant
Warner Brothers Store
F. W. Woolworth Company

A Changing Competitive Landscape

Way back when department stores were king, they were the main competition for everyone. Since department stores usually wanted at least keystone (50 percent markup or double the cost), margin and price weren't anywhere near as critical as they are today, and life was much easier for the independent. In the interim, since other, more cost-conscious forms of retailers (mainly discounters) now dominate the business, that has certainly changed. As well as I know the business, I was flabbergasted when I reviewed the sales volumes of the various retailers for fiscal year 2010 to see in cold, hard numbers the enormous shift with time.

According to *The Value Line Investment Survey # 11*, published by Value Line, Inc.,[2] on August 15, 2011, in fiscal 2010 the largest department store chain, Macy's, with all its stores coast to coast did $25 billion in volume.[3] The biggest home furnishings specialty store, Bed Bath & Beyond, did $8.8 billion,[4] while discounter Target did $67.4 billion,[5] and the biggest mass merchant, Walmart, did a whopping $421.8 billion[6] in volume!

But perhaps the biggest factor of all is the Internet. Today consumers don't even need to leave their home to buy almost anything they want, often tax-free and shipped at no cost. The traditional Internet retailers are gobbling up a larger and larger

2   Copyright©2011 Value Line, Inc. All Rights Reserved Worldwide. "Value Line, Value Line Investment Survey, Timeliness, and Safety are trademarks or registered trademarks of Value Line Inc. and/or its affiliates in the United States and other countries."

3   David Cohen, "Macy's," *Value Line Investment Survey #11*, August 5, 2011, 2143.

4   Garrett Sussman, "Bed Bath & Beyond," *Value Line Investment Survey #11*, August 5, 2011, 2169.

5   David Cohen, "Target Corp.," *Value Line Investment Survey #11*, August 5, 2011, 2152.

6   Kevin Downing, "Wal-Mart Stores," *Value Line Investment Survey #11*, August 5, 2011, 2153.

portion of the business. The ever-increasing impact of this type of retailer is already enormous, and it will undoubtedly only become a greater factor, forcing virtually everyone in the retail business to join the bandwagon and open a website.

An Evolving and More Demanding Customer

Customers are no longer loyal. Today's customers now shop where it is convenient and where they are more likely to find what they want, because their time is very precious. And yes, they have been spoiled to expect not only almost instant access and competitive prices, but also better and better prices. Sales! Sales! Sales! What have we retailers done?

When I entered retailing as a trainee on Bloomingdale's training squad in 1960, department stores were the undisputed kings of retail and set the standards for just about everything. Department stores were closed on weekends during the summer months; and their doors closed at 6:00 p.m. every night, except for Mondays and Thursdays, when they stayed open from 9:00 a.m. to 9:00 p.m. We lovingly called those days "iron days." Today most stores are open seven days a week for at least twelve hours a day. During the holiday season, some barely close at all, and in the last few days before a holiday, some don't close at all. I wonder what we should call these days! And, of course, the Internet is open 365 days a year, 24 hours a day.

Today the retailer must understand these changes and what they mean. But don't despair; with all these changes and challenges do come opportunities—ones on which the small independent retailer can capitalize to succeed and prosper.

You, as an independent retailer, have some very real advantages. You know your business inside and out, along with your customers—often even on a first-name basis. But most of all, your fate is in *your* hands, rather than under the control of a large organization. You are small and agile, with the ability to move much more quickly than your big competitors and take advantage of new opportunities as they present themselves.

I'll say in summary (and please note that I am painting with a broad brush) that to be successful in today's environment, you must develop a plan to continually respond to these changes and hone your retail operation to meet them and to capitalize on the ever-emerging opportunities. In other words, you must get better and better, more and more professional, and you must be ever vigilant for new opportunities.

You must continually do the following:

- Define your customer more precisely.
- Understand and offer what that customer wants.
- Work on all areas of the shopping experience to exceed the customer's expectations.

As part of this plan you must do the following:

- Constantly refine your vision or mission.
- Reevaluate your store layout, assortments, pricing, and marketing plans to maximize sales opportunities.
- Establish buying controls to better manage the business.
- Work with your vendors for better terms.
- Learn to use today's new technology to either serve your customers or communicate with them.
- Keep a sharp lookout for new opportunities.

I hope that this book will not only help prepare you for the task ahead but will help you to enjoy the fun and excitement of the retail game as well!

Chapter 2

Becoming an Independent Retailer

This chapter will explore two facets of being an independent retailer. The first is highlighting the main traits that most successful independent retailers exhibit; the second concerns the profitability of retailing and what an average independent shopkeeper might reap for his or her hard work.

Are You Cut Out for Retailing?

If you are already an independent retailer, chances are you exhibit many or most of the qualities I will discuss, and you can skip this chapter. Those of you who are thinking about becoming independent retailers, perhaps currently working for larger retailers and thinking of opening your own businesses, will find great value in the discussion (below) of attributes that are common among the most successful independents I have known over the years. While a few exhibited them all, most displayed at least a good many of them.

Above all, the most critical is to have the qualities of an entrepreneur. *Merriam-Webster's Eleventh Collegiate Dictionary* defines *entrepreneur* as "one who organizes, manages, and assumes the risk of a business or enterprise."

The most important questions to ask if you are an entrepreneur include, Are you a self-starter and risk taker? Do you want to be your own boss? Are you willing to tackle almost anything, including procuring the resources you need? Do you feel that you have a good chance of succeeding?

If you think you can answer in the affirmative to all of these questions, let's go a little deeper and examine these and other important inherent traits. To be a successful retailing entrepreneur you have to be a good multitasker, able to keep many balls in the air at the same time. You will need to be involved with merchandising and buying, financial issues, personnel and sales management, advertising and marketing, technology, and customer service.

Since it is difficult to be good at all these things, most large retailers divide the responsibility for these duties. Usually finance and operations are headed up by one person, and merchandising and marketing by a second. Often in a mom-and-pop independent, one partner is the merchant, while the other tends to the bookkeeping and store operations. Two partners share these skills, or the boss has a right-hand employee who exhibits what he or she lacks.

Of prime importance is whether you are competitive. This is essential because in retailing not only do you compete against your competitors, but your biggest competitor is yourself from the previous year, since retailers compare their daily sales to their sales from the previous year and hope, and usually plan, to beat them.

I vividly remember the first time I experienced the emotion caused by this practice. I had recently been made a buyer at Bloomingdale's and had just launched my first closeout promotion. By noon, that day was the biggest day that my department, the Bath Shop, had ever had, and I was ecstatic! Then a pall fell over me, and my enthusiasm was extinguished. I began to think, *What will I do next year to beat these figures?* Don't believe me? Just wait until you are a retailer, and you will experience this rather odd phenomenon.

Are you confident, self-starting, and self-reliant? You will be doing many things for the first time without a boss to ask how or where. It will be your business. Its success will be up to you, and you have to believe that you can do it!

How about decisions and problems? Are you good at making decisions? Do you have common sense? Do you consider yourself a problem solver? Do you enjoy the challenge of analyzing a problem and finding a solution—often a creative one? As an independent retailer, you will be making decisions constantly and independently, often under pressure. There will be a myriad of problems, some large and some small, which require your attention almost constantly. If you have trouble making decisions or are a second-guesser, retailing may not be for you. Furthermore, being creative will help you in any number of the tasks that will face you. Indeed, there are many who put creativity near the top of the list of attributes that successful entrepreneurs/retailers share.

Are you energetic, highly motivated, and healthy? In retailing at almost any level (including senior executives in large, well-staffed operations), there are never enough hours in the day because there is always something else that needs to be done. Long hours (often twelve hours each day, six or even seven days a week) will be your fate. Often, too, physical work such as moving the store around, schlepping boxes of merchandise, or being on your feet for long periods waiting on customers will require stamina and determination. Since the buck stops with you, being healthy enough to be on the job, or readily available most of the time, is usually important no matter what size the operation is.

Do you have good people skills? Are you an extrovert, and do you enjoy constant contact with people? You will be selling, handling customer complaints, dealing with suppliers, and directing a staff, all of which are a lot easier if you enjoy interacting with people and are good at it. As your operation grows, you will be hiring people, training them, and leading them. Your employees will be the key to your success—and the better you select and train them, the better your chances of a runaway success.

As was already mentioned, are you a risk taker? I want to be very specific here. Can you take calculated risks if the rewards are worth it? I am not asking whether you are a gambler or foolhardy by nature. Being a shopkeeper is like starting any other business. There are risks involved, and you have to be able to take those risks in stride.

But there are some risks in being a merchant that are not inherent in many other jobs. At the most basic level, for example, every time you select and purchase an item for your store, you are putting yourself on the line, taking the risk that someone will buy it from you so you will realize a return on your investment.

Furthermore, the fact is that many more retail start-ups fail than succeed. Do you have the stomach to put it all on the line?

Do you like predictability, or do you enjoy the unexpected? If you need predictability, then retailing is not for you. If you like the idea that every day is different, with new challenges, opportunities, and problems, and that you will always be busy because there is too much to get accomplished each day, then retailing is for you. I can honestly say that in all my years in retailing, I was never bored. I was always exhilarated by the ever-changing kaleidoscope that every day became.

Finally, do you have the necessary experience? If you are thinking of opening your own store, before you jump in, ask yourself whether you have any experience in retailing or in the products you are thinking of selling. The more you know about what you are contemplating, the better your chances of success will be. The closer your background mirrors the business you are planning to open, if nothing else, the easier it will be to get funding, if you need it.

Entering a new business merely because it is attractive to you is an almost impossible sale to the money people, and about as difficult to make a success. Before deciding to open your own store, consider carefully if you really have enough experience. If not, think about first working in the kind of store you want to open to learn as much about it as possible. Otherwise, you should strongly consider teaming up with someone who has the experience you lack or, at the very least, you will have one whale of a lot of research to do!

For example, just liking sports is not sufficient to warrant opening a sporting goods store. However, it could be considered one requirement, since liking the commodity with which you are going to deal makes things easier. It would be far better, though, to have helped manage a sporting goods store, and perhaps helped the owner with the merchandising. This experience would lend great credibility to your claim that you have some good credentials to support opening a sporting goods store of your own, and your chances of success would be greatly increased.

Experience at every stage of a retail business is at least a help, if not in some instances almost essential. For example, if your credentials are somewhat weak, but you are looking to expand your operation and need some financial aid, you may need to strengthen your story by getting a more experienced partner or hiring a seasoned employee. Or if your business is not doing as well as you want, you may want to take a similar action.

How Much Do Independents Make?

The answer to this question, of course, varies a great deal depending upon the classification and the success of the business. Usually most people are surprised by how little the average independent retailer makes at the end of the day, certainly at the beginning of the enterprise. After all, you buy something for a dollar and sell it for two dollars and pocket the difference, right? But this is only part of the picture. With the dollar profit, you must pay the expenses—and sometimes there is nothing left. As a matter of fact, while some do make good money from the get-go, many independents do not make any money at all (forgetting those who lose money, especially while getting established), but they do usually at least manage to pay themselves a modest salary and pay some other personal expenses, such as medical bills, out of the company coffers.

Value Line. Let's review what the most prominent public "big guys" (followed by Value Line, which publishes *The Value Line Investment Survey*) bring to the bottom line at the end of the year. Throughout this chapter I will use the fiscal year 2009 and fiscal year 2010 figures from Issue #11, released August 5, 2011.[7]

Value Line categorizes retailers in three general categories, while manufacturers that have retail stores are in other categories. The first category, Retail Store Industry, is composed mainly of mass merchants and department stores. These chains basically carry many categories of merchandise and are for the most part the largest retailers. Examples are Family Dollar, Kohl's, Macy's, Sears, Target, and Walmart stores.

The second category, Retail (Hardlines) Industry, is composed mainly of specialty stores selling items that are not apparel, like Bed Bath & Beyond, Dick's Sporting Goods, PetSmart, and Williams-Sonoma; the third category, Retail (Softlines) Industry, is composed mainly of apparel retailers, mostly specialty stores or cataloguers like American Eagle Outfitters, Chico's, Foot Locker, and the Gap.

The composite of the twenty-one stores in the Retail Store Industry in fiscal 2009 had a net profit margin of 3.1 percent of sales[8]; the Retail (Hardlines) Industry composite of thirty-two store chains produced 3.2 percent net profit[9]; and the Retail (Softlines) Industry composite of thirty-six stores had a much higher net profit margin of 4.6 percent.[10] However, the Retail

7   Copyright© 2011 Value Line, Inc. All rights Reserved Worldwide. "Value Line, Value Line Investments Survey, Timeliness and Safety are trademarks or registered trademarks of Value Line, Inc. and/or its affiliates in the United States and other countries."

8   Kevin Downing, "The Retail Store Industry," *Value Line Investment Survey #11*, August 5, 2011, 2132.

9   Michael Ratty, "Retail (Hardlines) Industry," *Value Line Investment Survey #11*, August 5, 2011, 2166.

10   Susan J. Ferrara, "Retail (Softlines) Industry," *Value Line Investment Survey #1*, August 5, 2011, 2199.

Store group produced much higher sales, $710.6 billion;[11] and the Retail (Hardlines) Industry sold $136.2 billion;[12] while the Retail (Softlines) Industry had the least sales: $98.4 billion.[13]

These are, I grant you, mind-boggling numbers, but they do serve to illustrate very poignantly that the larger discounters and department stores make less profit as a percentage of sales, but make tremendously more sales than the specialty retailer; so at the end of the day they obviously make more dollars.

One more thing to note before looking at the specific retailers: all these "big guys" have lots of revenue to pay their expenses, which shrink as a percentage of the total as the volume grows. The small independent retailer, on the other hand, must usually wait a few years before his or her expenses begin to shrink to any appreciable extent because of increased sales volume.

Retail Store Industry. Let's begin by reviewing the Retail Store Industry of department stores and discounters:[14]

RETAIL STORE INDUSTRY PROFITABILITY
FISCAL 2010

COMPANY	SALES ($MILL)	NET PROFIT ($MILL)	% NET PROFIT
Big Lots, Inc.	$4,952	$222.5	4.5%
BJ's Wholesale Club	$10,877	$135.8	1.2%
Costco Wholesale Corporation	$77,946	$1,307.5	1.7%
Dillard's, Inc.	$6,121	$168.3	2.7%
Dollar Tree, Inc.	$5,882	$397.3	6.8%

---

11   Downing, "The Retail Store Industry," 2132.

12   Ratty, "Retail (Hardlines) Industry," 2166.

13   Ferrara, "Retail (Softlines) Industry," 2199.

14   *Value Line Investment Survey #11*, August 5, 2011, 2153.

Family Dollar Stores, Inc.	$7,867	$358.1	4.6%
Kohl's Corporation	$18,391	$1,114.0	6.1%
Macy's, Inc.	$25,003	$867.0	3.5%
Nordstrom, Inc.	$9,310	$613.0	6.6%
J. C. Penney Co.	$17,759	$378.0	2.1%
Saks Incorporated	$2,786	$30.2	1.1%
Sears Holdings Corporation	$43,326	$231.0	0.5%
Target Corp.	$67,390	$2,830.0	4.2%
Wal-Mart Stores, Inc.	$421,849	$14,921.0	3.5%

As you will note, there is a wide swing between those that made the highest profit and those that made the least. Of these fourteen retailers, largely department stores and discounters, there were only three retailers that exceeded the 5 percent profit mark for fiscal 2010: Dollar Tree, Kohl's, and Nordstrom. And remember, these are the giants whose volumes help them the most in leveraging their expenses.

The small independent retailer would fit into the other two groups, the Retail (Hardlines) Industry and the Retail (Softlines) Industry. These groups are composed primarily of specialty stores, which have on average fewer stores and less volume, while producing on average a higher percentage gross profit than the Retail Store group but, of course, fewer gross margin dollars because of the smaller volume.

Retail (Hardlines) Industry. Next, let's review the specifics from the survey's Retail (Hardlines) Industry category for some of the best-known profitable "brick and mortar" retailers.[15] While most do have a web presence, they mainly do business from their retail stores, as opposed to those retailers whose business is primarily direct marketing with an occasional store.

---

15   *Value Line Investment Survey*, August 5, 2011, 2166–98.

RETAIL HARDLINES INDUSTRY PROFITABILITY
FISCAL 2010

COMPANY	SALES ($MILL)	NET PROFIT ($MILL)	% NET PROFIT
Bed Bath & Beyond, Inc.	$8,759	$791.3	9.0%
Best Buy Company, Inc.	$50,272	$1,424.0	2.8%
Big 5 Sporting Goods Corp.	$897	$22.1	2.5%
Cabela's Incorporated	$2,663	$121.3	4.6%
Coach, Inc.	$3,608	$734.9	20.4%
Cost Plus, Inc.	$917	$4.7	0.5%
Dick's Sporting Goods, Inc.	$4,872	$198.4	4.1%
Game Stop Corporation	$9,474	$408.0	4.3%
Haverty Furniture Company, Inc.	$620	$8.4	1.4%
Hibbett Sports, Inc.	$665	$46.4	7.0%
PetSmart, Inc.	$5,694	$239.9	4.2%
Pier 1 Imports, Inc.	$1,397	$100.1	7.2%
RadioShack Corporation	$4,473	$206.1	4.6%
Tiffany & Co.	$3,085	$376.4	12.2%
Williams-Sonoma, Inc.	$3,504	$200.2	5.7%

The overall profit for Hardlines is similar to that of the larger Retail Stores category, but a much smaller percent than that for the Softlines group—3.2 percent versus 4.6 percent. While many consider Hardgoods/Hardlines the hardest category in which to make a profit (no pun intended), there are, of course, many successful retailers in this category. As you will note in the fiscal 2010 listing of Hardlines above, the leader of the pack is handbag retailer Coach at a fabulous 20.4 percent profit, followed by jeweler Tiffany & Company at 12.2 percent—neither your garden-variety Hardgoods retailer—followed by Bed Bath & Beyond at 9 percent, Pier 1 Imports with 7.2 percent, Hibbett Sports at 7 percent, and

Williams-Sonoma at 5.7 percent; the remaining 60 percent of retailers brought home under 5 percent net profit.

Retail (Softlines) Industry. Finally, let's review the specifics with regard to some of the best-known profitable "brick and mortar" retailers from *Value Line's* Retail (Softlines) Industry category.[16] As was previously noted, it is generally the more profitable (and less complex) segment of specialty retailing:

RETAIL SOFTLINES INDUSTRY PROFITABILITY
FISCAL 2010

COMPANY	SALES ($MILL)	NET PROFIT ($MILL)	% NET PROFIT
Abercrombie & Fitch Company	$3,469	$150.3	4.3%
Aeropostale, Inc.	$2,400	$231.3	9.6%
American Eagle Outfitters, Inc.	$2,968	$206.4	7.0%
ANN INC. (Ann Taylor Stores)	$1,980	$76.9	3.9%
Chicos FAS, Inc.	$1,905	$115.4	6.1%
The Children's Place Retail Stores, Inc.	$1,674	$83.2	5.0%
Foot Locker, Inc.	$5,049	$173.0	3.4%
The Gap, Inc.	$14,664	$1,204.0	8.2%
Joseph A. Bank Clothiers, Inc.	$858	$85.8	10.0%
Limited Brands	$9,613	$805.0	8.4%
The Men's Wearhouse, Inc.	$2,103	$67.7	3.2%
Ross Stores , Inc.	$7,866	$554.8	7.1%
The Talbots, Inc.	$1,213	$40.6	3.3%
The TJX Compaies, Inc.	$21,942	$1,339.5	6.1%
Urban Outfitters, Inc.	$2,274	$273.0	12.0%

16   *Value Line*, 2199–2235.

As we can see, there is a very wide range of sales and profits among these fourteen publicly held companies. They range from 3.2 percent for the Men's Wearhouse to a spectacular 12 percent profit made by Urban Outfitters. It is most interesting to note that of the fourteen companies, nine (or 65 percent) made a net profit of 5 percent or better.

What Is an Appropriate Profit Goal?

So when the day is done, what should you hope for as an independent? Many feel that a reasonable goal for a young retail business is 2 to 3 percent net profit—or to say it another way, a reasonable goal for a store doing $400,000 is to make about $10,000 after taxes and all other expenses.

Before you turn up your nose at this amount, you should take into consideration that the business has paid the owner/owners a salary and some of their personal expenses. Furthermore, theoretically with each passing year as the business grows, you should be able to bring more to the bottom line and the business will be worth more—sometimes a fabulous amount eventually!

Virtually every large successful retailer was started as an independent shop by an entrepreneur. Obvious examples are Macy's, our largest department store chain, founded by Rowland H. Macy in 1858; and Walmart, the biggest retailer in the world, founded by Sam Walton in 1962. As the fourteenth-century proverb goes, "mighty oaks from little acorns grow."

Finally, a point not to be overlooked, you have the satisfaction of being your own boss and knowing that *you* have made the profit and it is *yours*—as is the future!

CHAPTER 3

Developing Your Mission and Competitive Edge

There are several critical elements in developing a successful business: the concept, the necessary funding, a marketing plan, and good employees. But every business starts first with an idea. In the beginning it is often difficult to know how good the idea is, but in time it will either prove itself or fizzle into oblivion. The most crucial step in starting or developing a viable business is to begin with a clear, well-thought-out concept, or mission, which is differentiated and hopefully has a sustainable competitive edge.

I highly recommend that you put your concept down on paper and formulate a clear mission statement that will facilitate your every step in the development of your business. Indeed, it will be the very foundation of your business. It will be essential to borrow money; it will be invaluable in attracting other personnel to your venture; and it will help to keep you on the path to a successful conclusion.

The Mission Statement Defined

Very simply, the mission statement is your store's reason for being. It describes your purpose, your niche in the marketplace, the focus of your business, and its aims.

Developing and refining your mission statement is such an important step in formulating a successful business; it will serve to clarify your thoughts and help you set a strategic direction to be effective in reaching your customers, and as you grow it will keep all your employees on the same page, which is vitally important in developing a consistent image for a successful operation.

Bloomingdale's Mission Statement. Let me illustrate the result of a great mission statement with a true story—the story of how Bloomingdale's became "like no other store in the world,"[17] a result that started with just a simple *idea*. This story is not well known today, but I know it because I joined the company right out of college nearly at the beginning of its turnaround, and I became a significant player in merchandising for the next twelve years. I was a firsthand witness to and participant in Bloomingdale's becoming "like no other store in the world."

Bloomingdale's was founded in 1872 on Manhattan's Upper East Side as a fashionable ladies' apparel store by Lyman and Joseph Bloomingdale. They strived to be first with their fashionable items and even established a buying office in Paris in 1886. The store moved to Fifty-Ninth Street and Lexington Avenue in 1929, just as the country slipped into the Great Depression, and within two years Bloomingdale's had expanded to fill the entire block and was acquired by Federated Department Stores.[18] As time passed, Bloomingdale's lost its cutting edge and downgraded, while the neighborhood in which it was located became more fashionable and exclusive.

One day in the 1950s two executives from Macy's—Jed Davidson, senior merchant, and Jim Schoff, senior finance man—were competitive shopping in other department stores in

---

17   Bloomingdale's, "A Brief History of the Most Famous Store in the World," *About Us: Press Release, July 6, 2007,* http://www1.bloomingdales.com/about/company/press/detail.ognc?newsID=70 (accessed April 6, 2012).

18   Ibid.

Manhattan. When they visited "Bloomies" (as it was called even in those days), they noted it was a real "schlock house," a bargain-basement kind of store, located in the richest residential area in the world. They wondered why the store catered to bargain hunters instead of the upper-class, rich customers who abounded outside its doors.

This realization led them to the idea of making Bloomingdale's a store commensurate with and for the wealthy neighborhood in which it resided. They went back to Macy's and added two other members to their team: Elaine McAlister, Macy's home fashion director, to develop a unique product offering; and Martha Scudder, the personnel director, to attract a new and vibrant team. The four left Macy's, taking with them their talents and their vision, and began their mission of making Bloomingdale's "like no other store in the world."

They would indeed change Bloomingdale's from a store filled with cheap, basic merchandise for the bargain shopper to a store of fashion-forward, unique, and exclusive merchandise for the upper-class, more educated, affluent customer (returning to its original roots, you might say) and effect one of the most dramatic turnarounds in retail history.

They put a new team in place (critical to their eventual success), trained them, instilled the new vision in them, and sent their buyers all over the world to develop a unique merchandise offering. Bloomingdale's attracted the best designers, found or created the most-wanted goods, opened breathtaking model rooms, and developed outstanding shopping bags that could be seen all over the world as part of their fabulous marketing effort. Bloomingdale's created retailing theater, all possible because of their crack team, all of whom were marching to the same drummer—their mission—which they all clearly understood.

Bloomingdale's exact mission statement of more than sixty years ago is probably long forgotten, but it may have read something like this: "Bloomingdale's will be a unique department store where the discerning customer will find the most fashion-forward, exclusive home merchandise and apparel from around the world for an unparalleled shopping experience and commensurate customer service." Bloomingdale's would be retailing theater and indeed become like no other store in the world. Their mission became well known, and soon a shorthand version became a slogan that would become ever-present in their advertising campaigns, "Bloomingdale's—like no other store in the world."

A well-articulated mission statement would have been critical in the development of Bloomingdale's because its new idea had to be communicated to all its employees, as well as to its vendors and its customers. There were lots and lots of people to tell the story to and make understand the new direction. But even in a small organization, indeed the smallest mom-and-pop retailer, a clear mission is essential for eventual success.

Sprenger's Sportsman's Depot. Sprenger's was the classic mom-and-pop independent's differentiated business. When I was a kid summering on Long Beach Island at the Jersey seashore, two blocks from our house stood the best example of an independent retailer's business with a clear mission and competitive edge that I have seen to this day. My twin brother worked there pumping gas.

The owner, Charlie Sprenger, was a great sportsman and an accomplished marksman and gunsmith. He was the sixth-best pistol shot in the world. On the main drag of Brant Beach, midway between the ocean and the bay, he built a sportsman's heaven. His big store had everything the fisherman, hunter, or boater would ever want, even small boats. (When I was eleven, my father bought a Barnegat Bay Sneakbox sailboat for me from Charlie's small boatyard adjacent to his store.)

When you entered Sprenger's Sportsman's Depot, you instantly knew where you were. Like Bloomingdale's, it was like no store anywhere—it was truly a sportsman's paradise. The huge store was divided into departments by sport, overflowing with everything anyone would want for that sport. All the walls were hung with Sprenger's trophies aligned with the sporting goods for that area.

Everything from a big stuffed bass that he had caught, to animals he had hunted—elk, caribou, bighorn sheep and mountain goats, as well as deer—adorned the walls and marked the spot for the appropriate sporting goods. The store was absolutely awesome and was like a museum or shrine for his youngest visitors, who accompanied almost every daddy.

In addition to Charlie's boatyard, he had a machine shop where he could fix just about anything for the sportsman, from guns to outboard motors. Out front, at the entrance to the store, were two gas pumps to service the sportsman's car or boat.

Sprenger's Sportsman's Depot was a one-stop shopping destination for his target audience, whom Charlie knew so well because he was one of them. His business was enormously successful because he was *the* authority. Whatever you needed to know about being a sportsman, Charlie knew and eagerly shared.

While I don't know if Charlie ever wrote a mission statement, it was abundantly clear; a shorthand version would have been "Everything for the sportsman!"

As an aside, the operation was also run as a classic mom-and-pop independent's business. His wife, Virginia, kept the books and did the more administrative stuff, while Charlie was clearly the chief guru and merchant.

Obviously, not everyone who wants to open a retail business has such a clear differentiator on which to base a mission statement, but one thing is just as clear: it is a good idea to discuss your ideas with as many people as possible who can give you input. The more you try your ideas on others, the more finely honed they will become and the closer you will come to developing a unique store for your target customer.

It is also important to note that for most companies the market and/or business conditions change over time, which will require revisiting your mission statement, probably every five years or so, to determine if it needs any adjustment.

In summary, then, a mission statement will define the organization and its reason for being. It identifies its primary customers, specifies the products and services it provides, and denotes its competitive advantages and business aims. The Bloomingdale's example illustrates this specifically:

- **what it is:** a department store
- **target customers:** discerning shoppers
- **products and services to be offered:** exclusive fashion-forward home merchandise and apparel
- **unique attributes:** unique merchandise from around the world
- **aims:** to offer an unparalleled shopping experience and commensurate customer service

Your mission statement will be the cornerstone of your business, so it will require a lot of thought and reflection, and you will have to shop and know your competitive landscape well. Once upon a time you could be successful by merely opening a shop; but to be a successful retailer today, you must find a niche in today's highly competitive marketplace that is not already taken, or address some aspect of your target customer's needs or wants that your competitors are not serving. The more unique the concept, the better chance you have of being successful—as long as your concept is not so unique that there is not sufficient demand for what you plan to sell.

Your Competitive Edge

Like Bloomingdale's and Sprenger's, do you have a competitive edge or USP? Your USP (unique selling proposition) is what sets your store apart from the competition. Your mission statement will be enhanced a thousandfold if it has a clear competitive edge. As an independent store owner, you have five main ways to develop this edge and differentiate your store. While your idea will rarely embody them all, the following are concepts to consider when designing your mission and mission statement:

- **Lowest Price.** As an independent retailer, you will find it is almost impossible to win here, because the big guys buy in such large quantities that they will almost certainly have lower prices and therefore the competitive advantage in this category.

- **Largest Assortment.** Here again it is usually difficult to beat the big guys unless you pick a small category, and then there may not be a large enough demand for it to support your store. But it is certainly not impossible, and if you find it, it can definitely be the key to your success.

- **Location.** The old retailing adage, "location, location, location," is intended obviously to suggest that one of the greatest elements to success is where your operation is located—and I certainly agree. If yours is the only grocery store located in a small town, you have a built-in element for success. As I have related, in the case of Bloomingdale's, this factor was what created and fostered the opportunity to become "like no other store in the world."

- **Area of Authority/Unique Assortment.** Here is where the gold is buried for the independent retailer (like Charlie Sprenger). What is the area in which you will profess to be an expert? How will that be reflected in your product line? How will your assortment be different from that of your competition?

- **Customer Service.** This is perhaps the easiest differentiator for an independent retailer. How you set your store up and how you deal with your customers should be entirely unique to your vision and can certainly set your store apart. A major emphasis here must be on the quality and training of your selling staff because they literally have the opportunity to make your store succeed or fail. They have the ability to enhance your concept, or they can drive your customers away.

Bloomingdale's mission encompassed several of the above differentiating elements. While location was the cornerstone of their idea or mission, combined with a great understanding of the customer who lived nearby, Bloomingdale's created a unique offering and concomitant customer service for that very affluent customer that propelled it to become an outstanding retail success.

Sprenger's Sportsman's Depot also encompassed several of these differentiators. While he was the authority, Charlie's operation also had a great assortment and fabulous customer service, and it was even located between the ocean and the bay on an eighteen-mile-long island!

As part of this process, it is important to concentrate on your customer.

The Customer. There are, broadly speaking, three different kinds of customers for whom to build your retail operation.

First, there are the *loyal shoppers*, who, unfortunately, seem to be almost a vanishing breed. They were the mainstay of both Bloomingdale's and Sprenger's Sportsman's Depot. Loyal shoppers have their favorite stores, usually specialty stores and some department stores, which they frequent. While never the largest segment of the customer base, loyal shoppers accounted for the greatest percentage of sales for many years. They are usually not price sensitive, care much more about good customer service, and particularly like all the little extras that make their lives easier, such as gift wrapping and delivery. Loyal customers like to be known where they shop.

On the other end of the spectrum is the *price shopper*, probably the largest-growing customer segment. These shoppers are motivated by the lowest price and have no loyalty to any store. They will often spend an inordinate amount of time to find the lowest price and go way out of their way for it. Their reward is feeling that they have really made a good deal and have not overpaid. They frequent, for the most part, mass merchants and outlet malls.

Expedient shoppers are those who go where they feel they can find what they are looking for quickly and get checked out fast. As time becomes more precious, this group of shoppers grows. They frequent all types of retailers and are rarely the ones who will shop till they drop.

Retailing was easier years ago when the loyal shopper was more the norm, because in many ways it was easier to get to know their wishes, wants, and desires and serve them accordingly. I remember when the Bloomingdale's customer came to the flagship store on Fifty-Ninth Street in Manhattan with a shopping list organized not only by floor and by department, but planned by departmental adjacencies as well, to expedite his or her shopping. Boy, was this shopper mad when Bloomingdale's started moving all the departments around periodically to give the customer a "fresh experience"!

But whichever customer type you choose to serve, Marshall Field's credo, "Give the lady what she wants," is as true today as it was when it was coined, and it is really the cornerstone of retailing. Your very success is dependent upon how well you supply what your customers want—or at least what they think they want.

The Mission Develops

As I have said, every business starts with an idea. Ideas develop into businesses differently depending on who develops them or sometimes just because of a nuance. Often they mature over time as well. The idea that became McDonald's mission is an interesting story that illustrates these points well.

During the summers of 1957 and 1958, when my twin brother, Greg, and I were teenagers, we worked for Burke's Barbecue, which was a drive-in hamburger restaurant with a very limited menu—mostly hamburgers, hot dogs, and French fries—on Long Beach Island. The food was made to order and competitively priced. Today Burke's still exists, under a different name, as a single mom-and-pop restaurant, surviving largely because of its excellent location on the main road of this beach resort.

About the same time, McDonald's was growing up in Chicago. As the story goes (used with permission of McDonald's Corporation, according to McDonald's US[19] and Canadian[20] websites), in 1940 two brothers, Dick and Mac McDonald, opened McDonald's restaurants, typical drive-ins featuring a large menu and carhop service in San Bernardino, California.

Eight years later (in 1948) they renovated their restaurant into a self-serve drive-in with a large assembly-line kitchen. The menu was trimmed to only nine items, with the mainstay being a hamburger reduced in price from a competitive thirty cents to only fifteen cents. *The fast-food industry was born.*

McDonald's was very successful, the brothers began to franchise it, and in 1952 they started advertising their concept in the trade magazines. In 1954 word of their rapidly growing business had spread widely. Ray Kroc, a fifty-two-year-old milkshake machine salesman (and high school dropout), visited them to find out why they were using so many of his Multi-Mixers. He hoped that once he knew this, he could sell even more milkshake machines to his other customers. He could not believe how many people they served so quickly, and he realized this business would succeed anyplace. While the brothers were looking for a national franchising agent, Ray decided his future was in hamburgers and became their franchising agent.

---

19   McDonald's, "McDonald's History—Travel Through Time With Us," *About McDonalds,* http://www.aboutmcdonalds.com/mcd/our_company/ mcdonalds_history_timeline.html (accessed July 16, 2011).

20   McDonald's Canada, "History," *McDonald's Canada,* http://www. mcdonalds.ca/en/aboutus/history.aspx (accessed October 2, 2011).

In 1955 Ray Kroc opened his prototype McDonald's, the same red-and-white restaurant designed by Stanley Meston (only smaller), in Des Plaines, Illinois. Kroc's McDonald's exhibited the winning formula of the original—a limited menu of quality food, assembly-line production for fast service, and friendly service—to which he added his own exacting standards of cleanliness.

As Ray Kroc later said, "If I had a brick for every time I've repeated the phrase *Quality, Service, Cleanliness and Value*, I think I'd probably be able to build a bridge across the Atlantic Ocean with them." [21] These continue as the McDonald's operating principles today, and every employee is steeped in them.

Kroc was growing the business fast (in five years there were 228 restaurants), but he realized that to reach its potential he would have to buy the brothers out of his very restrictive agreement. In 1961 he paid the brothers $2.7 million. The brothers paid their taxes, and each pocketed a million dollars. In that same year, Kroc opened Hamburger University for new franchisees and store managers to ensure his employees got the message and learned what they needed to know in order to run a very tight ship.

The rest of the story is like a fairy tale. By 1963 McDonald's "was selling a million hamburgers a day." [22] To celebrate its tenth anniversary in 1965, McDonald's had its first public offering at $22.50 per share. In 1966, one year later, Ronald McDonald appeared in his first national TV commercial, and McDonald's was listed on the New York Stock Exchange.

The growth of the company continued at breakneck speed. According to the company's Canadian website, "McDonald's broke the billion dollar sales mark in 1972 and the stock split for the fifth time, making the 100 shares of the original 1965 stock equal to 1,836 shares."

21   McDonald's, "The Ray Kroc Story," *McDonalds: Our Story/Our History,* http://www.mcdonalds.com/us/en/our_story/our_history/the_ray_kroc_story.html (accessed October 29, 2011).

22   McDonald's Canada, "History," *McDonald's Canada*, http://www.mcdonalds.ca/en/aboutus/history.aspx (accessed October 2, 2011).

In 1984 Ray Kroc died. That year McDonald's "broke the $10 billion sales barrier, served its 50 billionth hamburger and operated 8,300 restaurants in 36 countries."[23]

The openings got bigger and bigger, and the company grew by leaps and bounds. In July 2011, their US website stated, "McDonald's is the leading global food-service retailer with more than 32,000 local restaurants serving more than 64 million people in 117 countries each day. More than 80% of restaurants worldwide are owned and operated by independent local men and women," and McDonald's employed 1.7 million people.

Finally, their mission statement has evolved today to read, "McDonald's brand mission is 'to be our customers' favorite place and way to eat.' Our worldwide operations have been aligned around a global strategy called the Plan to Win centering on the five basics of an exceptional customer experience—People, Products, Place, Price and Promotion. We are committed to improving our operations and enhancing our customers' experience."[24]

This story illustrates better than any other I can think of three main elements to success: a unique concept or niche, an effective marketing package, and very specially trained employees. If you have these elements, everything else, including the funding for growth, will most probably fall into place.

I promised that this tale would illustrate how an idea can develop so differently given the person who develops it. In this instance the idea for the business was the McDonald brothers' idea, to which Kroc added his stamp of cleanliness and standards, along with his personal entrepreneurial management style. The originators ultimately sold the rights to the business to Kroc, who took the business and ran with it, working tirelessly until he died

---

23   Ibid

24   McDonald's, "McDonald's History – Travel Through Time With Us," *About McDonalds,* http://www.aboutmcdonalds.com/mcd/our_company/ mcdonalds_history_timeline.html (accessed July 16, 2011).

at eighty-one, a fabulously wealthy man who had developed one of the most successful businesses in US history.

In 2010 McDonald's total sales (including franchises) was over $75 billion around the world, while the former Burke's Barbecue continued as a nice little business on Long Beach Island. Let's look to the nuances and competitive edge that created vastly different levels of success. Other than Ray Kroc, there were and are two differences in the operations. At Burke's, the food was prepared to order and delivered to the customer nowhere near as quickly as at McDonald's, with its assembly-line techniques; and the hamburgers at Burke's were priced competitively, while those at McDonald's cost much less. Otherwise both establishments started out pretty much on the same foot!

In summary, Bloomingdale's took advantage of its location and built a better mousetrap for its affluent customers, with a unique assortment and fine customer service. Sprenger built a smaller business on his authority, large assortment, and personal service, while McDonald's built its mammoth business on price and customer service. All of these factors say that there are many formulas for a successful business, but there are only a few elements that make it up.

How to Develop or Hone Your Competitive Edge

Great mission statements range in length from paragraphs to sentences, although many marketing experts believe that no more than a few sentences should be adequate. To reiterate and summarize, the mission statement should be sharply focused, clear and easy to understand, realistic, and inspirational. Defining your company's niche in the market and its reason for being, your mission statement should clearly spell out who the customers are, what customer needs you are trying to satisfy, and how you will do so. It is your foundation and blueprint for success to help you motivate and inspire your whole organization as well as those with whom you do business. Some tips to help you write yours follow.

- **Collaborate.** While you can sit down in a room all by yourself and design your mission statement, it is vastly better to get a lot of input and be able to sort through a variety of ideas and suggestions before "casting your new mission statement into bronze," as they say. If your business is established, it is vital to include your employees in the process to ensure they buy into it. Brainstorming sessions can often reap results you could never have imagined. If you are just starting out, talk to as many people as you can who can give you good input. Also, your prospective vendors can often be most helpful in this regard.

- **Study your competition.** Review your competitors' strengths and their weaknesses, either looking for gaps that you might fill or being sure that you have a more differentiated edge.

- **Review other mission statements.** There are a great many books written on the subject, but I think your best source for help is the web, which has many articles on the subject. In addition, since so many large organizations will not give their approval to reprint their copyrighted mission statements, I can't include some of my favorites here, but Googling "great mission statements" will yield more than you will ever care to read. One particularly notable site is http//www.makingafortune.biz/, which includes mission statements for the Fortune 500, even categorized into segments such as "top retail companies." While, as time goes on, some of them have changed, you will get plenty of ideas from them. Obviously, your object is not to find one to copy, but to get a feel for how others have written them, and to be inspired by them.

- **Take your time.** The mission statement is an important document for your company's success, and it shouldn't just be slapped together. You want it to guide your company for at least the next few years, and it will be as good a guide as it is a well-thought-out plan.

- **Answer five basic questions.** Either in a group of associates, or after a thorough discussion with others about the basics of your concept, ask the following five questions (one at a time) about your business, and write down all the answers you get.

  1. What will make your operation different? (Pricing, location, assortment, customer service, etc.)
  2. Who is your customer, what are the needs you want to satisfy, and how important will your differences be to them?
  3. How will you accomplish your aims and make these factors more important or obvious?
  4. How easily can the differences be copied by your competitors?
  5. How will you communicate the differences to your customers?

- **Prioritize and review the answers.** Prioritize the answers to each question from best to worst. Determine if any can be combined for greater strength of the concept or shortened. Then select the best.
- **Put it all together.** Not all entrepreneurs are wordsmiths, but most are relatively fearless. This is the one time when, if you are not particularly literate, you should pull the concept together—no one can as well as you— but then find a friend, or a professional, to polish it into its final form. You want it to be descriptive, realistic, inspirational, and distilled to a couple of sentences that describe your business's reason for being. Not only do you want your mission statement to hit the mark, but above all, you want it to be easy to remember.

- **One final review.** Before finally accepting your company's mission statement, take it for a test drive. Try it out on employees, friends, and vendors to see how they react, to be sure that it is creating just the impression you had in mind. Remember, this is not a document just for you; it is to help guide your business and explain it to a myriad of other people. If something needs refining, take the time to do just that. I promise you, you will be glad you did.

The Vision Statement and the Value Statement

While smaller businesses usually define their missions with a single mission statement, some larger companies write two other statements in addition to their mission statement: a vision statement and a value statement.

The Vision Statement. This is a broad statement, often one line that explains what the company aspires to become in the future. The vision statement is often incorporated into the mission statement; but when it is a separate statement, the company's mission statement confines itself to who the company is, what the company will do, and how the company will do it—or simply why the company exists.

For example, consider CVS's mission: "We provide expert care and innovative solutions in pharmacy and health care that are effective and easy for our customers."[25]

Compare this with the company's vision statement: "We strive to improve the quality of human life."[26]

---

25   CVS Caremark, "Our Vision, Mission & Values," *CVS Caremark,* http:// cvscaremark.com/ourcompany/ourculture/vision-mission-values (accessed July 13, 2011).

26   Ibid.

The Value Statement. One additional statement often added by large companies is a value statement, which describes the traits or core qualities that are crucial to them in running their business—in other words, their guiding principles.

CVS's values as articulated on the company website are as follows:

- **Accountability**
  We take ownership for our actions and the results.

- **Respect**
  We treat customers and colleagues so they feel valued and appreciated.

- **Integrity**
  We do what we say and what is right.

- **Openness**
  We try new things that will lead to innovation.

- **Teamwork**
  We share information and resources as we work together to deliver results.[27]

I do not believe that a separate vision statement or value statement is necessary for a young business, or one starting out, but to reiterate, I do think that every business, no matter what its size, should definitely have a mission statement. The reward for a well-thought-out mission should be a vastly better chance of success and, ideally, greater profits!

---

27   Ibid.

CHAPTER 4

Writing Your Business Plan

Why Write a Business Plan?

While many entrepreneurs do open businesses without formal business plans, I believe this is foolhardy. Whether you are starting a business or are already in business, the business plan is a key element in increasing your chances of success. A business plan is a written document that states the purpose, goals, and objectives of a business; includes the planned strategies to achieve them; and gives projections, including the financial aspects of starting/building it for its future. The plan communicates the strategic vision of your company to those you want to know.

They say nothing succeeds like a plan. To try to open a business without one not only is taking a chance, but it might even be impossible. Furthermore, you should consider your business plan to be a living document, reviewing it often and updating it yearly to keep your business on course and deal with any important new developments that may arise.

The process of writing the first business plan normally takes at least several weeks, but most people find it was well worth the effort when it is completed. While it does take time in the beginning, it usually helps businesses avoid mistakes, some of which could be catastrophic, later on. The process forces you to do a lot of research, and a lot of thinking, analyzing, and reevaluating as you systematically work your way through the plan.

There are several important reasons to write a business plan, especially if you are contemplating opening your first store.

It helps you improve your concept and your chances of success. In writing the plan you will really need to do your homework to logically substantiate your concept and prove your case with cold, hard facts and numbers. Throughout this process you will be doing a kind of feasibility analysis. Along the way you will probably uncover areas of weakness that need to be improved or threats that have to be overcome before your concept can reach its potential, which should be incorporated, with the solutions, into the plan. It also becomes a reality check. In extreme cases, you might even find that there are too many obstacles to be successful and decide, before losing any more time or money, to abandon this concept and look for another.

It is the road map or blueprint to keep you on track and help you make sound decisions as you build your business. To create an effective plan, you will have to study the business from all angles and chart a course of action to grow the business and avoid the many pitfalls along the way. While you may later occasionally deviate from your plan, it should not be on a whim but only with real justification (perhaps because conditions have changed), because you have already painstakingly and logically set your course.

It can serve as a major communication, selling, and motivational tool as you build your business. It will describe and "sell" your concept and company not only to potential investors, but to future partners, employees, and suppliers as well. It can also be used as an important motivational and training instrument for everyone in your organization.

It will set the goals for your company in the short term and for several years out, which will form the basis on which to evaluate your company's performance and success or lack thereof.

Finally and most importantly, it is unlikely you will be able to raise any money without one unless, of course, you have a fairy godmother or a friend or relative who believes blindly in you and your mission. If you opened your enterprise without a business plan and at some point in the future need significant funding to grow, you will almost certainly need one then.

The purpose of this chapter is not to make you an expert on business plans. Rather it is intended to familiarize you with the subject and perhaps encourage you if you are thinking about opening a business, improving the one you have, or attracting some additional funding, to at least start the thought process that leads to creating one.

There are many ways to write a business plan, and scads of books have been written on the subject. There are professionals who will write one for you, as well as many software programs on the market to assist with developing a business plan. For the most part these programs are sophisticated and require a good deal of input, but you may want to go this route. In addition, the SBA (Small Business Administration) and SCORE (Service Corps of Retired Executives) have business plan outlines and write-ups on the web that arc very good, as well as business plan templates that you might want to consider to guide you through the process.

Whatever course you choose, however, I really believe the best one is the one for which you must do the lion's share of the work yourself—that is, the conceptual work and the research. If you leave the guts of it to someone else, you may not be able to spot the pitfalls or answer those difficult questions that a reader, perhaps your intended investor, is bound to ask later on.

As you begin your plan, not only will you find that it requires a lot of thought and research, but you may well find that you also need some help from a financial person who is more facile with the financial information that should be included, and/or from a friend in a similar but noncompeting business. If you are not a wordsmith, getting some help from someone who is may be a good idea, because usually the more professional the document is, the better the chances of its success. This is the time to do the research, get all the help you can, ask all the questions you can, and find the answers. I cannot stress this enough—the more thought-out your plan is, the better your chances for success, no matter what the stage of your business!

General Rules for a Business Plan

Before I discuss the content of a business plan, let me mention some general rules that are important in making a professional one:

- **It should be as brief as possible, while telling your story completely.** The text should be only a few pages, but the appendix, which contains substantiating facts, can be as long as necessary to make your case.
- **Make it compelling and persuasive**, but easy to read.
- **Confirm that it is well researched and complete** with all the reader needs to know.
- **Be sure the facts and claims are accurate and substantiated**, not exaggerated.
- **Include a title page, a contents page, and numbered pages.**
- **It should be neatly typed and simply formatted, and it must contain no typos or grammatical, mathematical, or spelling errors.** Have someone else proof it for you. It is impossible for most people to do an adequate job of proofing their own text because they know so well what they have written that their minds tend to overlook the little errors. (I must confess I learned this the hard way when writing my first book, and it caused me a good deal of embarrassment.)

Inserting your plan into a three-ring binder or having it bound also makes it look more professional.

What Should the Plan Include?

The following segments of the plan are necessary for your first plan and will simply be updated for subsequent plans. If you are writing a plan for an already established business, it is easier because so much of what you will be including is history rather than projections. The order of the items will vary by the writer's preference, but the following segments should be included:

    I. Executive summary
   II. Company description/history
  III. Products, services, pricing, and competitive advantage
  IV. Market and marketing plan
   V. Management and organization
  VI. Operations plan
 VII. Funding request (if applicable)
VIII. Financials
     A. Income statement
     B. Cash flow statement
     C. Balance sheet
  IX. Appendix

I. Executive summary. This is usually the last thing written since it must encapsulate the main issues of the entire plan in a dynamic one-page (or at most, two-page) document meant to give a basic understanding of your concept/company and convince your reader to read the entire plan. Therefore, *it is the most important part of your plan.*

The executive summary contains your mission statement and briefly but enthusiastically outlines your concept, products/services, targeted customer, management team, and your credentials; why your concept is exciting; why it will work; any major risks and how they will be minimized; and, if appropriate, what you want your reader to do (e.g., invest). If you are already in business, it will also encapsulate the history, current investors, any noteworthy accomplishments, position in the market, and future plans.

II. Company description/history. This section should position the business you intend to open or discuss your present business.

Business description. Begin with a brief description of the industry. Then flesh out your company's mission, describing the business's size, scope, and products/services; how your business will fit into the overall business world (its niche and uniqueness); where it will be located; the customers you intend to serve; and what problems you will solve for them. (Some of these will be discussed in greater detail in the following pages of your plan.)

Goals and objectives. This section is the place for any company goals, objectives, and principles you have formulated.

Structure of the business. How is it, or how will it be, organized (sole proprietorship, partnership, corporation)?

III. Products, services, pricing, and competitive advantage. This can be a fairly brief section, but it should clearly and simply discuss your offering.

Products and services. What kinds of products are you selling and what services do you offer (or plan to), and how do they compare with those of your competitors?

Pricing strategy. Describe your pricing philosophy and strategy (to be discussed at length in the next chapter) and how it does, or will, equate to that of your competitors.

Competitive advantage. As was discussed in the previous chapter of this book, what is your USP (unique selling proposition) or competitive edge? What problem does your concept solve, and what makes it different from the competition? Although this has been introduced earlier in your business plan, here is the place to discuss it in depth, since this is one of the key points that any investor will be looking to find and assess in evaluating the potential of the business.

In the Bloomingdale's example, what was the underlying problem that the store would solve for its prospective customers? Simply, the neighborhood shoppers would be able to shop in a store that catered to their tastes. Furthermore, its unique assortment, tailored just for them (USP), would set the store apart from its competitors.

In the case of Sprenger's Sportsman's Depot, the store was a one-stop shopping destination for virtually anything the sportsman needed, whether it was equipment or advice. The store's USP was that sportsmen needed to go nowhere else.

McDonald's solved the problem of good, fast, and very affordable food, and its USP was that it did it faster and more cheaply than anyone else.

The harder your concept is to copy or duplicate (this is known as the barrier to entry), the better your chances for success and for a buy-in from investors.

IV. Market and marketing plan. This section consists of several segments.

The market. How large is your target market? Describe your market using appropriate statistics for substantiation and credibility. Is it a growing market, a contracting market, a fragmented market, or a niche market?

The supply chain. How will you procure your products? Can you get as much product as you need easily? Are there any government regulations or other factors to be concerned with?

The competitive landscape. Who are the major competitors? How successful are they? What are their strengths and weaknesses? How will you, as they say in marketing parlance, be positioned against them?

Trends in your business. Describe the current trends and any that are likely to have an impact on the business over the next few years. Consider trends in the market, product, pricing, and competitors. Are there lifestyle changes and taste changes that might affect the business? (For example, if you are opening a tabletop/gift store, the continual move to more casual dining is one you must address; if your store is a men's shop, the shift to casual attire for the office is another key trend that will certainly affect anyone in this business.) Above all, don't forget technology and the impact it might have on your business.

The target customer. Define your customers as closely as possible, using both demographics and psychographics. In a nutshell, the better you know and can describe your customers, the more closely you can tailor your operation to cater to their wants and needs, and the more successful you are likely to be. This will also require some serious research, since you will need relevant statistics about your target audience: How many of your target customers are there? How often do they purchase your type of goods? Where do they reside; what are they like? What motivates them to buy? The bottom line is that you must be convinced, and you must be able to convince your business plan reader, that there are enough of your target customers within your marketing area to create a successful business.

Marketing to your customer. First, how will you distribute your products? Will it be via stores only? Adding a website? By mail? Some other way?

Second, how will you reach your customers? This is another one of the most critical aspects for success. To open your business and to build your business, you must get the word out to potential customers.

Not only do you need to understand the basic message that you want to communicate to your target customers, but you must also understand the best ways to reach them, which will naturally be greatly affected by your marketing budget. With an unlimited budget there are numerous different ways to communicate with your customer, while with a much smaller budget, which most independents have, the choice is more limited. Advertising on television, in most newspapers, and through direct mail (mailers and magazines) is either not affordable or, because of the costs involved, can be used only for very special events. However, on a more limited budget there are still many other effective ways to advertise, such as public relations campaigns, special events, bag stuffers, coupons, and newsletters, which are used by retailers of all sizes and will be discussed at length in the chapter 11 discussion of advertising. In addition, with the advent of the Internet, you have an increased possibility of communicating with your customers very affordably. I will discuss Internet marketing in chapter 12.

In your plan you must cover this topic completely because potential investors will look at this segment very closely. Without a sound and reasonable marketing strategy your plan will be considered suspect and will be very difficult to sell.

While this segment may require a lot of research, it is one that gives you the opportunity to really come across as knowledgeable about the business and the customer, or conversely, to look ill prepared. But even more important, it is an area that you must thoroughly understand because it will be a major element in your success.

V. Management and organization. This section also contains several important segments.

Your personal background. In this section you introduce your credentials as they relate to your proposed business. Highlight your education, experience, and anything else that is germane to selecting this as a business and enhancing your ability to make a success of it. Specifically, what experience and/or skills do you have that are relevant to this business? What evidence of past successes can you exhibit?

Management team. If you have others joining you, introduce your management team and other significant personnel in depth. As was previously mentioned, very often the key players might be a husband-and-wife team, in which one partner is the merchant and the other is the bean counter. These are the two sets of skills that you will have to convince your reader that you have covered, one way or another. If you are the merchant, as the founder of a retail company often is, perhaps in the beginning your accountant can play the role of the financial/operating partner.

In this section include a small biography of anyone who is joining your management team, highlighting his or her specific background and accomplishments, especially regarding how they relate to your chosen business.

Other personnel. In addition to the merchant's vision and knowledge of the business and a financial person's talents, personnel with the following skills are generally needed as well:

- marketing (advertising) skills
- personnel management skills
- operational know-how (concerning the running of the business)
- legal knowledge

These can often be absorbed by the merchant, the finance person, and one of their lawyers in the early days of a business, but they should be addressed. However, additional selling help is often required almost from the beginning, and this should be noted along with how you will recruit any other personnel needed.

The stronger the management team, the more likely you will be to raise the money you want and, in general, the better your chances of success. Indeed, many believe that this is the most important section to any potential investor.

Organization chart. If you plan to have a large enough organization, it is a good idea to include an organization chart. It should convince your reader that you have analyzed your needs thoughtfully and that there is a fundamental logic to your plan, as well as to the responsibilities each member of the team will have.

Board of directors. While many small independent businesses do not have boards of directors, if you have one or intend to have one, it can be a real plus, and the members should be introduced here, along with their credentials.

VI. Operations plan. This segment describes the resources you will need to set up and operate your business, how you will run it, and all the costs involved. Depending on the scope, complexity, and developmental stage of the business, you will go into as much detail as needed to ensure your readers' comprehension.

Selling requirements. If you are opening a retail business, you will describe your physical selling space needs, desired location, and storage and inventory requirements. If you are expanding the business, your immediate and future needs should be detailed.

Vendors. Describe the vendor community from whom you will source your products.

MIS (management and informational systems). Discuss the kinds of management and informational systems you will use.

The web. Here you should also explain how you will use the web in connection with your business if you will be selling from it.

VIII. Funding request (if applicable). In this section, if you are requesting funds for starting up or expansion, you will flesh out your request very specifically—how much you want over what time period and how will it be collateralized, as well as how the funds will be used and for what.

IX. Financials. Now it is time for the statistical segment, the part where you are to convince your prospective investors or new partners what's in it for them—or convince yourself that this undertaking is worth pursuing. Bottom line, you need to show how successful this business will be. Will there be enough cash to repay any debt, withstand dry periods, and sustain and grow the business?

Let me say at the outset, without acceptable forecasts (or acceptable recent financials for an ongoing business), it is unlikely that you will be able to borrow any money. By the same token, unless you are good at and comfortable with math, you do need to get someone to help you with these, preferably an accountant with some familiarity with your business. If the financials are inadequate, flawed, or unrealistic, it will be very difficult to get buy-in.

If you have been in business, you should supply financial information for the last three years. If yours is a start-up, all the necessary financial statements will be pro forma, meaning projections. The general rule is that you should forecast out at least three years, but the first year usually gets by far the most emphasis.

There are at minimum three financial statements necessary for a business plan:

The twelve-month income statement. This is often referred to as the profit and loss statement, or P&L, and it is the financial document that summarizes the company's revenue and expenses, and determines whether the business has made, or will make, a profit or suffer a loss.

Net Sales – Cost of Goods Sold = Gross Profit – Expenses = Net Profit or Loss

The statement starts with revenues (sales minus returns), deducts the cost of goods sold (merchandise plus freight), which nets the gross profit dollars available for paying expenses. Next is a listing by major category of all expenses; this figure is deducted from the gross profit, which results in either a positive sum (profit) or a negative amount (loss). For the first year it is generally done on a monthly basis with an annual summary; for years two and three, the calculation is completed on an annual basis only.

This is the most important document in deciding whether to proceed with a new business or to make an investment in an existing business, so it requires great diligence and accuracy.

An example is provided in chapter 13 of this book, and there are lots of examples and even templates available for a P&L on the web that can help you with the process.

The balance sheet. This is a snapshot in time that lists all the company's assets, liabilities, and shareholders' equity for a particular day. It is used to determine a company's worth. For a start-up it is a pro forma balance sheet, usually the last financial document prepared, and lists all the values on opening day. For an ongoing business it is normally prepared annually at the end of the fiscal year. The formula is as follows:

$$\textbf{\textit{Assets = Liabilities + Shareholders' Equity}}$$

Assets are the items of financial value; these can be physical, like inventory or cash, or nonphysical, like trademarks. Liabilities are debts owed to creditors, which include all obligations like loans, debts to suppliers or employees, and taxes owed. Equity is the worth that remains for the shareholders/owners after the debts are subtracted from the liabilities.

It is called a balance sheet because the assets must equal (or balance) the sum of the liabilities and shareholder's equity, which are the means (borrowing or from owners) by which the company has paid for its assets.

The cash flow statement. This statement complements the income statement and the balance sheet and is an important document because it forecasts your sales, your available cash to pay your bills (credit sales take some time to produce cash to pay bills with), and your monthly outlay. For a start-up, this analysis forecasts if you can get through your first year.

For a more established business, it summarizes where the company's money came from and where it went. The statement generally reviews the cash flow from three segments of activities: operating, investing, and financing. Since it shows how much cash the business is generating, it is a prime indicator of the company's health.

Given by month for the first year, the cash flow statement shows your estimated total revenues (sales) and those funds that are available to pay bills (cash and any accounts payable due), and then subtracts the amount of the monthly fixed expenses and the amount of other invoices due that month. If the remaining figure (to be carried over into the next month) is in excess, it indicates there will be funds to pay invoices due that following month. A negative amount, on the other hand, signals that you will not be able to pay the bills due for that current month and leaves the deficit amount to be made up the following month. (For years 2 and 3, the figures are annual.)

Like all the forecasts you present in your plan, they should be as well thought-out and realistic as possible, but *this one is particularly important to ensure that you are properly funded to begin your business and that you will have the money to pay your monthly bills.*

Although there are many templates on the web available to create the cash flow statement, this is a complex document, and I believe unless you are financially savvy you should seek an accountant's aid in preparing it.

X. Appendix
Be sure to include in your appendix anything that will help your cause, such as the following:

- surveys/articles on business conditions
  - market research studies
  - census/demographics
- articles from newspapers, magazines, or the like about your existing or proposed business
- copies of leases or proposed lease agreements
- construction plans and permits
- renderings or photos of your building
- resumes of senior managers
- contracts and other legal documents
- listing of key business advisers, including attorney and accountant
- anything else needed to support the plan

It should be noted that often much of the information included in your appendix is confidential, so in such cases, the appendix should not be included in the body of your plan, but should be made available for those with a need-to-know status, such as potential investors.

Where Can You Find Help?

In addition to the people you know, today with the advent of home computers and search engines almost anything you need to know is accessible on the Internet. It just takes a little time and some effort. Needless to say, there are a myriad of companies on the web advertising to write your business plan for you, but having had no experience with them I cannot comment. However, in addition to libraries, there are some websites and other sources that can be particularly helpful in your research:

US Small Business Administration (SBA). The SBA provides free help, counseling, and information to small businesses and entrepreneurs through its Small Business Development Centers (SBDCs), which are partnerships between the government and universities and colleges. Their website (http://www.sba.gov) is excellent and includes a wealth of information, with write-ups on just about every subject of interest for anyone contemplating starting a business or trying to improve one. The site also includes extensive write-ups on business plans, including all the templates and forms you might need, as was already mentioned. Another section on their site (http://www.sba.gov/content/general-business-statistics#) provides access to just about any statistic one could want. The SBA is one fabulous resource.

SCORE. The Service Corps of Retired Executives, which uses the tagline "Counselors to America's Small Businesses," is a resource partner with the SBA and also has a great website (http://www. score.org) and outline for writing a business plan, plus all the forms you might need. In addition, they have over twelve thousand volunteer counselors (not all retired) across the United States to help entrepreneurs start a new business or grow one. They hold over eight thousand seminars a year and have forty online workshops. SCORE is another marvelous resource that offers their services at no charge.

Trade Associations. These associations exist for an amazing number of businesses and can be a real help. They range in size from the NRF (National Retail Federation), which is the largest retail association in the world, and its affiliate the Retail Advertising and Marketing Association to much smaller, more specifically targeted ones like the National Sporting Goods Association, the American Craft Council, and the Museum Store Association. You can find a very extensive listing of trade organizations at http://www retail. about.com/; search "trade organizations."

Trade Journals, Magazines, Newspaper Articles. Publications that are dedicated to your chosen business are also great resources. The *Entrepreneur* magazine website has an extensive list for retailers of all kinds and levels (http://www.entrepreneur.com; search for "retail trade directory"), as does the Warrington College of Business Administration (http://www.warrington.ufl.edu; search for "retail trade publications").

Competitors. Other companies in your field are a wealth of information. They can teach you a great deal about the business with their brochures and catalogs, as well as through visits and conversations, which are very enlightening, both as you research a business and when you are in business.

Suppliers. Conversations with vendors who know a great deal about the business and the competitors can usually be of great aid in helping you amass information.

Customers. Your customers can be very helpful, especially if you are seeking some specific information like details on their wants and desires, how they feel about a competitor, or feedback about some aspect of your own store.

My Promise to You

Granted, writing a business plan sounds like a lot of hard work—and it is. But I will promise you, having myself written business plans and faced major venture capitalists for millions in funding, the security you will feel when you have worked your way through writing your plan is your first large step toward success. A well-thought-out business plan can not only help you get the necessary resources and avoid future pitfalls, but also should be your road map to greater profits.

CHAPTER 5

Conveying and Enhancing Your Mission

As was discussed in chapter 3, the main ingredient of successful retailing is a clear-cut mission that emphasizes a unique selling proposition or competitive edge. A number of elements help to convey and enhance your mission, and the skillful application of these can make all the difference between success and failure. The most obvious are listed below:

1. Location
2. Store design and ambience
3. Store pricing
4. Customer service
5. Communication of your mission through advertising

I will discuss each of these as they pertain to expressing your mission, and also in some depth because all play a significant role in creating and maintaining a successful operation. I will start with location—perhaps the most important decision you will make after determining your mission or business concept.

Location

We have all heard the retail adage that the most important keys to success are location, location, and location; like many adages this one has much more than a grain of truth to it. Location is a tremendous contributor to success or failure. First, it conveys to your customers a lot about your vision or mission before they even enter your store. (Please note that in this section I am addressing retail stores, not catalogers or Internet sites.)

But even more important, are you situated, or planning to be situated, where the type of customer you want normally shops? Perhaps the single most important element for you as an independent is to make sure your location is, or will be, situated in a trading area that contains a substantial number of your targeted customers. If it isn't you have an uphill battle and you will have to stimulate your traffic with extra marketing and advertising, which, of course, translates into extra expense.

Locations come in several different retail configurations, which have their own unique advantages and disadvantages, and often vastly different customer bases and cost structures as well. Obviously, finances will often play a major role in this decision. The key for you as an independent retailer is to strike a workable balance between which are the most practical or feasible and where you would ideally like to be. While there are a number of ways to categorize these retail configurations for "brick and mortar stores," for simplicity's sake I will classify them as downtown, stand-alone, shopping center, kiosk, and home locations.

Downtown. Usually considered a premium location, downtown offers a much higher degree of freedom for the retailer than the mall or shopping center. Often downtown is populated by older, more established stores. Here your store will be able to draw from a lot of people, especially the office trade, but parking can be a problem, and all downtown locations are certainly not equal. Normally there is a chamber of commerce, which helps to bring traffic to the town and can also be quite useful in other ways to the independent retailer.

Stand-Alone. Freestanding buildings that house businesses are referred to as stand-alone locations. They usually offer you, the retailer, the cheapest rent and the greatest freedom in operating your business, but the trade-off is that you must attract all your own customers, since there may not be neighbors to help.

Shopping Centers (Malls and Others). These large collections of stores located together and developed by one group, account for a tremendous amount of today's retail activity. There are several types and ways of classifying them, but for our purposes I will keep it very simple. However, if you want the official definitions for each type, the International Council of Shopping Centers publishes the ICSC Shopping Center Definitions, available on their website (http://www.icsc.org) and which they update periodically. In addition to the definitions, ICSC has included for each concept relevant statistics such as how many of each type there are, their average size, the number of anchors, and the size of their trade area. A detailed look at each major type is below.

Malls are a special type of shopping center in that they provide access to all their stores through a common entrance or entrances, and they offer plenty of parking for easy access. Considered premium space, they generally have the highest rent per square foot. Malls are built around several anchor stores (often department stores) that bring in a healthy traffic flow, but they are also home to chains, independents, and even kiosks, so there is a lot of variety to entice the shopper to visit.

Depending on their size, regional malls generally draw traffic from within about fifteen to twenty-five miles and are usually directed toward a specific set of demographics, which can be a distinct advantage. Selecting space in a mall inconsistent with a business's target audience will spell disaster.

Finally, the mall offers you the least freedom in running your business because lots of rules and regulations must be adhered to—like specific opening and closing hours, which create long days that can be very arduous for independents.

Local shopping centers have rules like the mall, but they are usually not as stringent. Generally, access to each store is though its own entrance, and, unlike in a mall, to enter another store you have to go outside. Most communities have several shopping centers of various sizes and configurations. Larger shopping centers are composed of a number of freestanding buildings that may house one or more retailers and often will have an anchor like Walmart or Target.

Power centers are larger shopping centers that have several big anchors and a number of freestanding store complexes.

Off-Price or *outlet centers* consist of value-oriented retailers, mainly factory outlet stores and department store closeout outlets. They normally have lots of stores and draw from a long distance.

Lifestyle shopping centers are among the newest and trendiest shopping centers. They are populated by a certain type of store, usually not as mainstream, which together act as a draw for their normally upscale and affluent customer base. Some call it a boutique shopping concept. The ambience and setting are very nice and warm, usually with tree-lined paths and lots of fountains and ambient music.

Strip centers are a collection of small stores, often housed in a single building, having separate entrances but sharing a parking lot. These shopping centers have lower rents, live on local traffic, and offer convenience shopping.

In addition to the locations already listed, there are a couple more that are the most affordable, especially for a small business or one starting out:

Merchandise Kiosks. These provide small temporary locations in enclosed malls, train stations, airports, and office buildings and are suitable for a myriad of small businesses.

Home. A retailer's own home is the simplest of all retail locations and is often used in start-up situations to see if the concept has merit. While being in one's home can be a bit confining and limiting, it can be useful in determining a "go or no-go" situation. In addition to the myriad of service businesses that we can think of that are often run from home, there are also any number of product-oriented retail businesses that can be home based, like making and selling gift baskets or jewelry, or holding Tupperware parties.

Among the most nostalgic and well known of these retail operations is, of course, the lemonade stand that neighborhood kids start on their front lawns during the summer. They are expressing the most idyllic kind of retailing. Whatever they sell is pure profit because Mom usually provides the supplies and lemonade. When they grow up later and start a retail business, the process is nowhere near as simple, but they may have gotten a good taste for the game during those summers!

With all these choices, you might ask, "What is the best one?" Of course the answer will vary with the circumstances, but broadly speaking, *the ideal location is one you can afford, where you are near to and easily accessible by your target customers, where you find the rules and regulations acceptable, and where you are among stores serving customers similar to yours.*

Some might think that the last thing you would want is to be near or, even worse, next door to a competitor for fear the competitor would steal business from you. While this is a natural fear, experience has shown me that the result is quite the opposite. When I was a specialty retailer (working for Workbench and Dansk), my very best stores were always those located close to a competitor, because their advertising and foot traffic provided extra traffic for my stores and vice versa. And since we were offering our customers different assortments (of essentially the same categories of merchandise), our customers had more to choose from with a kind of one-stop shopping. You might say we (and they) got double the bang for the buck.

There are many factors to consider when selecting a spot for your store, and many elements that combine to make a good location. Whether it is your first store or a new one, you will be constantly learning as you visit new sites. This is a complex issue, and some of the best retailers are known to have made serious mistakes from time to time.

Obviously, before beginning your search, it is important that you know very clearly what business you are running or are going to run, what kind of a customer it will serve or you are serving, and what your strategic objectives are. But I also recommend that you get aid from a local real estate agent or consultant. A good professional who knows the area and the kinds of customers who live there can save you a tremendous amount of effort and help you enormously in making the right decisions. The key considerations follow:

- **Demographics.** The customer base must come first. Is the property located near where your targeted customer lives or works, and is the population pool sufficient to support your business plan?
- **Accessibility.** Is the space easy for your customers to reach? Is sufficient parking available? Can your suppliers make their deliveries to you easily?
- **Space.** Can you envision your operation in the space? Is there enough room for whatever you need? Can the space be laid out the way your business will require it to be? Is the entrance appealing? Are the heating, lighting, and ventilation sufficient for your needs?
- **Labor Pool.** Will you be able to hire the quality and number of workers you require?
- **Competitors.** Are there any competitors nearby (with whom you think you can compete successfully) that could enhance your operation by bringing additional traffic? Are they doing well enough to add confidence to your selection of space in that area?

- **Lease.** Are the lease terms acceptable and within your budget? I strongly recommend that you get a good real estate lawyer to negotiate your lease terms and check the zoning laws to ensure that you will have no problems. More often than not, a real estate lawyer will save you far more than you will pay him or her.

Store Design and Ambience

Your store itself conveys more about your vision than any other single component. Bringing customers into your store is like inviting guests into your home. Does the overall impression reflect your mission? Does everything about it solidify your strategic message? If you are selling diamonds, does it look like Tiffany's? If you are selling merchandise for the student or starter household, does it reflect the simplicity of an IKEA? Does the ambience reflect the mission and the targeted customers, or are there some elements of the environment that are discordant and detract from, rather than promote, your mission? These are the questions you must ask yourself and remedy if the answer requires it. You must consider all the elements, with respect to both design and ambience.

Your Store Design. This framework sets the stage for your store's ambience, your customers' shopping experience, and their perception of your operation. There are many important elements:

The Storefront (facade and windows) begins the customers' experience and, as the first thing they see, is vitally important to their overall impression. Although often you do not have much control over the structure of your store's facade, make sure when selecting a store that the front is something you can live with, and that at least will not distract from the overall message you want to convey to your customers.

Windows, if you have them, are not only important from a design point of view, but they are also a major communicator to your customers. They say the eyes are the windows into a person's soul; similarly, your windows provide a glimpse into what is inside. You should ensure that all aspects, from the merchandise selected, to the props and the backgrounds, are commensurate with and supportive of your mission and what you want your customers to feel. They should also be changed frequently enough to keep them fresh and make customers stop to see what is new rather than just walk by because they have seen it all before.

Your signage, especially your store name sign, should reflect your mission—graphics and font should be trendy if your store is trendy, traditional if it is traditional, and so on—but above all, it must be legible. One of the biggest errors some storekeepers make is developing a store name logo so intricate or embellished that no one else can read it.

All store signage is an integral part of communication with your customer and stands ready to communicate a consistent message to your customer when no one is around. It should help your customer on every level—from clear departmental signage to direct her on her way; to product signage that helps her learn more about your wares and their pricing; to customer-service messaging that spells out your store's position on the various important issues.

Merchandise signage and pricing should be clear and easy for the customer to find and comprehend. Nothing is more frustrating than to find a piece of merchandise that interests you and there is no price on it. You have to track down a salesperson, who sometimes has to go and find the price while you wait for a vital piece of information that should have been readily apparent.

Your store layout should also be reflective of your mission. If you want the store to be gracious and easy to shop, categories should be clearly defined and aisles should be wide enough to allow easy passage, while all the merchandise should be in plain view and readily accessible. If, on the other hand, you want to achieve a feeling of "the hunt" for your customers, the layout should be more cluttered and the merchandise not all so easy to see at a glance. Always remember who your customer is, and "decorate" your house for your intended guest.

The fixtures should work for the merchandise and be made of materials that are appropriate for your mission. They should also be of a quality commensurate with that of the merchandise you sell. For example, if the store's fixtures are appropriate, sturdy, and well maintained, it subliminally telegraphs quality for your merchandise; however, if the fixtures are tacky and falling apart, they will communicate to your customer that your merchandise may follow suit—an impression that is certainly not good for business.

Ambience. In addition to the major design elements we have just discussed, which contribute so significantly to the feeling of your store, there are others (some also technically design elements) that deserve special consideration because their real power is often overlooked.

The colors (walls, floors, fixtures) should reinforce the mood and your mission. Softer or more neutral colors suggest one kind of mood, while bolder and brighter colors suggest quite another. Traditional colors, for example, telegraph a feeling of classic security, and avant-garde or fashionable colors project a bolder and more modern sentiment.

The lighting should set the tone for the store. Few elements are so capable of expressing and enhancing the feeling you want to communicate. Some believe it is the single most important element, though I would not go quite that far. I have often thought of lighting as colors on a painter's palette. Different types of lighting and varying intensities should combine like colors on a painting to make the shopping experience what you want for your customer. Obviously, ambient lighting will be quite different from the spotlights you might use to highlight your displays and quite different also from the lighting in a dressing room or restroom.

Music, if any, should amplify the mood you are trying to create. In addition to selecting the right kind of music for your store, choosing the right intensity is also very important. Playing music too loud is a definite no-no and can be very effective in driving customers (except possibly teenagers) out of the store.

Displays are your silent salespeople and one of the most important tools for communicating with your customers. They should tell provocative stories, include cross-merchandising for add-on sales, and allow your customers to visualize how these items can be used, often in a multiplicity of ways. They should be eye catching, created thoughtfully, kept fresh, and changed often to create a vibrant impression.

Bathrooms and fitting rooms are crucial to a customer's impression of your store and to your customer service. Every effort should be made to make these areas as appealing as possible and to keep them that way. Obviously, keeping them clean is paramount. I am always amazed at how relatively few retailers put the proper emphasis on these areas.

Housekeeping is a critical, sometimes almost overlooked element in making a favorable (or otherwise) impression on your customers. This is not just a matter of keeping dust to minimum, but it extends also to overall neatness and maintenance of all areas, especially the checkout area, where you hope the customer will linger long enough to get the lay of the land. Stained rugs, dirty ceiling tiles, scuffed-up paint, and burned-out bulbs will distract mightily from the overall ambience.

Store Pricing

Pricing Philosophy. One of the first things a retailer must decide is what the company's overall pricing philosophy is (or will be) and how that fits into the spectrum of the market. If you know what kind of a store you have, or want to open, the choice is usually obvious, as these policies should absolutely reflect your store's mission. It is the everyday execution that can be more problematic because pricing each new item appropriately requires a good deal of knowledge and judgment.

Joel Evans and Barry Berman of About.com Retailing note the three most fundamental choices: high-end, medium, or low-end.[28]

28   Joel R. Evans and Barry Berman, "Pricing and Small Retailers: Questions to Consider (Part2)," *About.com Retailing*, http://retail.about.com/od/productpricing/a/pricing.htm. (accessed April 5, 2012)

Retailers with a *high-end (or premium) pricing philosophy*, typically used by fine specialty stores of all sizes, are banking on their reputation, product offering, customer service, and ambience to allow them to price their goods above the market. Conversely, with a *low-end (or discount) pricing philosophy*, typically used by mass merchants, retailers feature below-market prices, usually because their operations have lower operating costs and/or they can buy advantageously (closeouts, odd lots, and so on).

With the *medium (or competitive) pricing philosophy* used by most department stores and independents, retailers are not using pricing as the main competitive factor, but rather price the goods consistent with the market and build their competitive advantage on other factors like product assortment, customer service, or store ambience.

Adhering religiously to one's pricing philosophy is very important because inconsistent pricing with prices all over the map simply serves to confuse the customer. Also, with time, your customers will begin to know where your store stands vis-à-vis the pricing, and this will absolutely influence them as to when and for what they come to your store.

Pricing Strategies. After the main pricing philosophy has been decided, a number of combinations of pricing strategies are possible. Keeping it simple, consider these four fundamental pricing policies:

- **Everyday Low Pricing.** Across the board this strategy is usually chosen by larger retailers that are established enough not to need to hype their businesses with sales; also these companies buy in large enough quantities to assure everyday low prices that are attractive to the consumer. This policy reflects great legitimacy in pricing and is a comfort to the customer, but it is usually not practical for the smaller retailer, except possibly in the case of some basics.

- **Regular (Full) Price without Promotions.** Selling consistently at full price (except for clearance) is usually the domain of the very exclusive retailers, like Tiffany's. It presents the most prestigious impression and, of course, ensures the legitimacy of their pricing. Like everyday low pricing, it avoids the problem of customers feeling cheated when they have just bought an item and then see it advertised on sale. But also like everyday low pricing, it does not permit the retailer to stimulate extra traffic or volume by running a sale.
- **Regular Price with Promotions.** This is perhaps the most widely used of the pricing policies because, when properly used, it keeps legitimacy of the pricing and allows the retailer to hype the business when necessary with sales. The caution here is that too many sales (which are very addictive for the results they can produce) will cause customers to begin to disbelieve the normal pricing and wait for the next sale. This has taken many a retailer down.
- **High-Low Pricing.** Each price tag at high-low retailers shows a higher comparison price (or an inflated retail price) and a sale price at which the item is now selling. This policy is typically used by retailers who want to present an aggressive pricing policy and almost suggest an everyday sale posture, but this is often rightly mistrusted by the consumer.

Many retailers use a variety of pricing strategies depending on whether the item is a commodity, an exclusive, or a fashion or seasonal item. Many specialty stores use everyday low pricing for basic items; regular price for exclusives; regular (full) price with occasional sales for fashion and seasonal items; and clearance sales for all. Administered correctly, this approach achieves a good balance of customer confidence in pricing and the ability to hype the business when necessary with a sale.

Pricing Methods. After you have selected your pricing strategy, there are a number of methods for arriving at the retail or initial selling price of each item. Correct pricing is one of the most important keys to profitability. In any of the aforementioned strategies, if prices are too high, items will not sell as well as they could; and perhaps, depending on the competitive climate, items may not sell at all. In this scenario shopkeepers often conclude that there is something wrong with the items, rather than acknowledging there is something wrong with the pricing. Conversely, if an item is priced too low, it will probably sell out quite quickly, but you will have shortchanged yourself on the profit you might have made with a slightly higher price. While there are many pricing methods, I will discuss briefly only the most common.

MSRP (manufacturer suggested retail price) is often used by independents. The MSRP is a retail price made and recommended by the manufacturer. This has its upside in that it makes retailers look competitive in their marketplace, keeps them from having to decide on the pricing, and usually sets a high enough price to provide a decent profit. The downside is, of course, that retailers can't stimulate the sales by sharpening the price, nor can they take advantage of the opportunity for extra margin, if it is there, by raising the price.

Keystone pricing is perhaps the best known of the several costing methods that utilize the *cost* of the item in establishing the final retail price. With this pricing method you merely double the cost to arrive at the retail or selling price. However, this method is not used as much today as in the past, because many items/markets have become too competitive to allow what amounts to a 100 percent markup on cost, while other markets have become so expensive that they require an even higher markup to make ends meet. A friend of mine who runs a successful fashionable gift shop starts at keystone and then either adds or subtracts some to arrive at his retail price, which is a price that "feels" right to him. And this seems to work well for him.

Markup on cost is a method in which the retailer has figured how much he or she needs to earn (as a percent of cost) to cover his or her overhead. As an example, let us assume our retailer has decided he needs to earn 80 percent over cost to cover expenses and make a small profit.

Therefore if the item costs $15, the shopkeeper needs to add $12; that is ($15 × 0.80) to sell the product for at least $27 and make his predetermined markup. To figure the markup on cost, he would use this formula:

Markup Amount ÷ Item Cost = Markup Percentage

$$\$12 \div \$15 = 80\%$$

I can vividly remember when I became buyer for my second department. The previous buyer (quite famous in those days) had left a markup sheet that showed for every dollar of cost what the retail should be. When a new product arrived, she went right to this sheet. Whatever number was across from the cost number on her chart automatically became the retail price. While this made pricing an item simple (and some retailers do it this way), to me it is seriously flawed in that, like keystone pricing, it doesn't preclude retailing a product either too high or too low—either way preventing an item from reaching its true profit potential.

Markup on retail/selling price, used by larger retailers, is a variation on this theme. With this method the retailer views his or her markup as a percentage of the selling price, and markups usually vary from item to item and from classification to classification.

As an example, our retailer is going to purchase an item for $15, and he thinks $27 is a good price to sell it for.

The calculation here is as follows:

Markup Amount (Selling Price – Purchase Price)
÷ Selling Price = Markup Percentage

$$\$12 \ (\$27 - \$15) \div \$27 = 44.4\%$$

Note this is the same cost and the same selling price as in the example above, yet because it is figured on the *retail* instead of on the *cost,* it becomes a lower percentage. Confusing, huh? But that is the way it works.

While this method of calculation does make the markup percent sound less, the main advantage of this method, in my opinion, is that it allows the retailer to more readily focus first on what each particular item can bring to maximize its potential, and then determine if that markup will be sufficient for his needs. With this method the retailer works with varying markups, some higher and some lower (as noted above), rather than determining what markup he needs and fitting the retail into that formula. Of course, at the end of the day, he must be sure that his total markup for his items will average enough to cover his cost of goods and expenses with some left over for profit; so he must know that percentage and keep it in mind when retailing his goods.

While pricing this way does demand a good grasp of the pricing in one's market, done right it allows the retailer to be competitive and also make that little extra when he can to offset being sharper where he has to be. In my opinion, this is really the essence of merchandising and can be a key ingredient in enhancing profits.

Granted this method is subjective, but whether to buy and offer a product is subjective as well. Since it is so subjective, I recommend that, in cases where you are uncertain, you ask others for their opinions (those whose opinions you value, of course). This is a case where two may see more than double, and the reward can be extra profits for pricing items at a level your customers find appropriate!

Competitive pricing by retailers requires them to price their wares in relation to their competition—for example, with lower discount pricing—and decide their retails based on the retail prices around town rather than starting from cost. To be successful, they either have to get sharp prices from the vendors or have low-overhead operations to make up for the lower return they get on their wares.

Other Pricing Issues. There are several other issues concerning pricing that are worthwhile to mention in a discussion on pricing.

Dollar endings refers to the cents at the end of each price; that is, whether a price ends in .99, .95, or .00—like $9.99, $9.95, or $10.00—and it is yet another pricing decision retailers must make. Even pricing, ending the dollars in .00, is the most exclusive method and is usually used by the upper tier of retailers. More mainstream retailers usually use .95, while the more promotional houses usually use .99. Many retailers will use .95 for everyday pricing and .99 to distinguish any sale items, which I think clarifies the pricing nicely for the consumer.

It should also be mentioned that the .99 ending is often used in what is termed psychological pricing because it is believed by many that $9.99, for example, will mostly be perceived by the customer as $9.00, rather than $10.00, so he or she will believe the item is cheaper than it really is.

Knowing the merchandise total cost is critical if you are basing your retails on cost. One of the biggest errors I have seen over the years is that a buyer will often set the retail based on the manufacturer's invoice cost and forget about any other amounts that should be either added to or subtracted from the first cost to arrive at the true cost of the item when it lands in your store.

The biggest additional item that is usually overlooked is freight. Freight, especially on small quantities or larger items, can turn out to be an enormous percentage increase on an item. It normally isn't forgotten on very large items like furniture, because the freight can be up to, and sometimes even in excess of, 100 percent of the seller's cost.

I will never forget the day I placed my first order for a container of rattan peacock chairs from Cebu in the Philippines. Each chair cost fifteen dollars, and when I figured the clearance charges and the freight to get it to the United States, it totaled an additional $14.97, so the true landed cost would be just under thirty dollars! Had I keystoned the chair for thirty dollars, I would have made virtually nothing on any chair I sold. Instead, to make keystone I had to retail it for sixty dollars (or $59.99 or $59.95, depending on my preference for dollar endings).

Discounts reduce the landed cost of an item and, theoretically, should be deducted from the cost before the retail is set. However, unless you can expect to get the same discount in the future when you order the item, it is wise to just forget about it. Otherwise, you will be either shortchanging yourself in the future or have to raise the retail because your cost will be higher on your reorder.

Even though you may choose not to deduct discounts when you set your retail, I strongly recommend that before agreeing to purchase any item, you remember to ask if any discounts are available. I have found that this is another area which buyers tend to overlook, but if one pursues discounts rigorously, they can amount to a substantial amount of money in the course of a year.

An in-depth discussion of the types of discounts and allowances that are often available appears in chapter 8, "Utilizing Vendors More Effectively."

The bottom line here is that to make a profit, no matter what system or systems you use for pricing your goods, you must understand all your costs well enough so that you price your merchandise high enough to cover all the costs of both procuring your merchandise and running your operation.

Customer Service

This is a critical element that speaks volumes about your store to your customer. For you as an independent retailer, customer service can be one of your greatest tools in differentiating your store, attracting customers, and developing loyal customers.

I cannot stress enough the importance of constantly shopping your competition to ensure that your policies are competitive and stay that way; you should also continually search for that special customer-service edge that might lure a customer away from your competitor to you.

Your store policies are critical in setting the proper tone and should reflect your store in every way. They should be written down formally, and your salespeople should be thoroughly trained in all aspects of your customer service.

Return Policy. Your store's return policy is perhaps your single most important policy. The bottom line of any return policy is to assure your customers that if something goes wrong with their purchase, they have some recourse and will be treated fairly.

Ensure that your return policy offers the same (or better) guarantees as your competitors. If, as an example, none of them offer cash refunds but issue store credits instead, then you are on safe ground doing the same. However, if each one offers a cash refund within ten days, and you don't, you will be putting yourself at a real disadvantage. Obviously if your competitors offer only store credits and you offer cash refunds as well, you will have a competitive advantage.

Your return policy should be posted prominently in your store. Be careful about the wording of your return policy to ensure that it is as positive and comforting as you can make it. Signs that read No Cash Refunds or the like can be a real turn-off to customers, while, as some have suggested, a sign saying, If something is wrong, we will make it right, is reassuring to customers and makes them feel that they have some recourse if there is a problem. Needless to say, this is a promise that you must follow through on. Failing to honor it will undoubtedly lose your customer.

Make your return policy explicit. If, for example, you require a receipt for an exchange or return, your sign should say so. If you want to limit how old an item can be before you take it back, your policy should specify so (e.g., "Returns must be made within sixty days.").

Credits, Exchanges, and Complaints. It is critical to make sure your staff is well trained in handling these. Give your employees guidelines for handling the situations, so they can settle the more routine matters, while keeping the ones you are needed for to a minimum. Try to have someone in the store at all times who can make whatever decisions are necessary. While this may not always be possible with complex issues, access to you by cell phone when you are out of the store might save the day. Nothing is more annoying than to go to a store to resolve a problem only to find there is no one there who can help you.

I must stress that how you and your staff deal with returns and other complaints is of paramount importance. You have undoubtedly heard the customer-service saying attributed to Marshall Field's: "The customer is always right." But it is sometimes difficult to keep that in mind. It is very easy to become jaded after you or your salespeople have experienced some pushy customers who, for example, want to return merchandise that is so old you don't even carry it anymore or damaged merchandise that they have clearly damaged themselves.

I recall vividly being livid when I was a young buyer at Bloomingdale's and a customer, a very famous singer, tried to return an extremely expensive hand-embroidered organdy tablecloth that she had obviously used and soiled. Righteously, I turned her down only to be overruled by the customer-service person posted on my floor, who was less concerned with the profitability of my department than she was with keeping the customer for the whole store. This customer would ultimately be more profitable for Bloomingdale's than the small loss my department would sustain on the one returned item.

The lesson I learned was that, often, winning the battle with a customer can be a Pyrrhic victory. You may win your point but lose the customer. Now, I am not advocating being taken undo advantage of; I am simply suggesting that, although handling returns and other complaints effectively and diplomatically will probably require more diplomacy and sagacity than anything else your business will demand of you, it is worth working at. Customers are hard to come by, so saving one without giving the whole store away is a worthwhile goal.

Other Store Policies. Careful thought should be given to the issues below, and details should be prominently posted in your store:

- **Hours of Operation.** Normal hours of operation, including extended store hours, if any, for holidays, as well as any days the store may be closed.
- **Payment Types.** Credit cards and foreign currencies accepted, as well as identification or other information required of customers paying by check.
- **Layaway Purchasing Terms**, if allowed.
- **Special-Order Requirements**, if applicable.

These policies should not be carved in stone but should be monitored against those of your competition on an ongoing basis to help you remain competitive and even allow you to gain the upper hand.

Employees' Attitude and Conduct, Appearance, and Product Knowledge. These elements are crucial not only to your store's image but also to delivering good customer service and satisfying your customers.

The attitude and conduct of your employees is of utmost importance. Those who are cheerful and exhibit a real desire to help or solve a problem will undoubtedly be your top salespeople. They will be very effective because wanting to help is at the very core of customer service. A positive attitude, good communication and listening skills, plus a willingness to go the extra mile, are the basic tools in providing a good shopping experience for your customers; and they will go a long way toward making your customers feel important, a major goal in customer service.

Little things will make your customers feel welcome or turn them off. Make sure, for example, that your employees greet your customers as they enter your store and thank them for their visit or purchase when they leave the store.

It is even better if you and your salespeople can get to know your customers and address them by name. It sounds like such a little thing, but here is a case in point: There is only one dry cleaner at my summer home at the Jersey shore, and he is taking full advantage of the situation by charging extremely high prices, which I find somewhat annoying. But since I do have to have some clothes dry-cleaned, I put up with it. Whenever I enter the store, the man behind the counter always greets me with, "Ms. Bradshaw, how are you this fine day?" Somehow I never feel as bad paying the bill after that!

Train your salespeople not only to answer a ringing phone immediately but also *how* to answer customer calls and respond to basic customer questions. There is little that is more annoying than to call a store for some information only to find the answering machine is on, or to get an employee who can't answer the most basic questions.

Employees should look neat and properly attired. Many retailers find it helpful to make employees more visible by having them wear something special like a particular shirt, something the store sells, clothing in a special color, or an apron with the store's logo on it. But if you have no special store attire, your employees should still be neat and clean, appropriately dressed, and well groomed. They are your ambassadors and will be huge contributors to the impression your customers will have of your business.

Your employees' product knowledge is a major key to good customer service. Knowledgeable assistance may well be one of the main reasons that your customer is coming to you rather than to a mass merchant. The more your employees know, the more professional and expert your operation will appear to be. Many people are more than capable of deciding what they want to purchase if they know what they need to know about it. However, few will buy an item if there is something they need to know and no one is available who is capable of answering their questions. This is why almost all retailers, regardless of size, spend a lot of time teaching their employees their FABs—features, advantages, and benefits—and why many stores develop training programs and training books to continually increase the level of their salespeople's proficiency and expertise.

While these sound like simple commonsense things, they make a big difference, and you would be surprised to find out how often they are overlooked. Check them out on your next competitive visit.

Special Services Enhancing Your USP (Unique Selling Proposition)

Whatever your specialty, USP, or area of authority is, you should give great thought to how to embellish it and capitalize on it with your customers through special customer services. Often referred to as value-added services, these can tremendously increase your store's overall image and strategic advantage.

Special ordering items that you don't stock but that are important to your store's vision can help increase your perceived range of goods and expertise with little or no investment.

Private-label merchandise, items made for you with your store's name on the product or label, is an excellent way of increasing your authority. Although minimums are often high, whenever it can be afforded within the merchandise classes you carry, it is an excellent way of adding prestige or, depending on how you price it, a value image to your store.

"How-to" classes and demos such as cooking demos, gift-wrapping classes, or sessions on how to select the perfect gift, for example, not only add to your perceived authority but, since they are usually held in your store, serve the dual purpose of increasing traffic.

Product consultants, salespeople who have particular expertise in a category you sell, can offer these services to your customers. For example, a salesperson who is a great cook can not only speak authoritatively on cookware, but can also offer cooking suggestions to her customers. Or a gift salesperson who is especially good at recommending gifts for various occasions or who is talented at wrapping gifts can offer these services to your clients.

Private showings or shopping hours for your best customers can give sneak previews of next season's items at a special time. Keep a list of these customers' interests and call them when you have a new shipment of merchandise that they might like. Or have a special shopping night before a holiday when you can give your best customers complete attention for their shopping needs.

Giveaways and samples can make a great impression on customers because everyone loves something free. Many of your suppliers will supply free samples of the items you buy, such as scents or food items. If you scatter a few of these freebies throughout the store, it will lead your customer on a tasty or fun treasure hunt and should produce extra sales of the items sampled.

Assembly assistance can make a difference if you sell any item that needs to be assembled. Offering to assemble it for a customer, even at a cost, is a great customer-service move and can often make the difference between making the sale or not.

Delivery service—either offering to mail customers' gifts for them (for a cost) or making home deliveries for them—is another way of making your customer service very appealing.

Gift registries for the bride and groom and also tailored to your operation for other individuals or occasions (for baby, for Christmas, for birthdays, whatever) are a great way of binding your customers closer to you and making them more loyal to your shop.

Gift wrapping is one of the most powerful weapons of all. Keep it simple and as affordable and representative of your store as possible. It is best if you can build its cost into your markup so you can offer it for free. This is an enormous plus for any store that sells gifts. But since there are few stores that do not sell any number of items for gifts through the year, this idea is applicable to many stores, not just your traditional gift store.

As part of this program, it is important to offer gift boxes, which can be hot-stamped with your store's name and logo in reasonable quantities and at affordable rates. What a pain it is to find a lovely gift and then have to go elsewhere to find a suitable box to wrap it in. While many items lend themselves to gift bags, just as many don't. It is surprising how many larger chains don't offer gift wrapping at all and how much business this could ultimately cost them.

It is also relatively easy to have ribbon stamped with your logo. The boxes and the ribbon are good examples of private-label merchandise that add prestige to your store and extra value to gifts from your store.

Gift sets or gift baskets offered as part of your gift program are another excellent way of setting your store apart and establishing you as an expert in your area. Food baskets, wine and cheese baskets, and other edible goodie baskets come to mind immediately; but there are few stores that cannot find items in their assortment to be combined (either in a vessel or wrapped in gift paper or cellophane) to make very appealing gifts. While some retailers (Williams-Sonoma is especially good at this) make baskets/sets ahead of time and display them throughout the store for easy customer "take-withs," others will combine items that a customer selects and gift wrap them in one package to make a very individual gift statement.

This is just a partial list of special services that can be added to your store to differentiate it and garner loyalty from your customers. With a bit of thought you can come up with others that will fit your operation perfectly, enhance your image with your customers, and result in extra sales and profit dollars.

Conveying Your Mission through Advertising

Direct Mail, Catalogs, Fliers, and All Internet Communication. These modes of communication all convey your image and mission directly to the customer and should therefore be of a quality that is consistent with your store. Obviously a classy store should send a classy statement no matter what it is about, while a budget store should ensure that the quality of its mailings reflects its cost-consciousness as well. A classy statement from a budget store would only serve to confuse the customer, as would an obviously cost-saving mailing from an upscale retailer.

Needless to say, when, where, and how you advertise says a lot about your store. If you select the media that are right for your store, chances are you will reach the customer you want to reach. I will talk much more about advertising later in chapter 11 ("Getting the Word Out") and chapter 12 ("Utilizing Internet Marketing"). Suffice it to say now that all aspects of your advertising should adequately reflect your store and sell your store as well as the merchandise you are promoting.

Store Events. When these are run as part of your advertising campaign, they are a tremendous marketing tool for the independent retailer and can greatly enhance your mission as well. Whether they are clearance, sale, or charity events, how you design and run each will tell your customer a great deal about you. Properly conceived and executed, they can get lots of free publicity, create goodwill, and produce extra sales; sloppily run, they will be a detriment. I will also talk about them in greater depth in chapter 11.

CHAPTER 6

Shopping the Competition to Hone Your Competitive Edge

Your Competitors

Competitors can be of invaluable aid to you in honing your competitive advantage and showing you the way to increased profits. It never ceases to amaze me how many retailers do not recognize the importance of shopping the competition. After all, can there be anything much more important than strengthening your competitive edge? How better to do it than by visiting your competitors and evaluating their operations?

Who are your competitors? Everyone knows a competitor is a rival. Many retailers think of their competitors as the other small independent retailers, usually those in his or her town. While this is certainly true, the larger retailers who sell whatever you sell are your competitors as well and perhaps your fiercest ones. Furthermore, it is often from them that you can learn the most. While some suggest zeroing in on the three retailers most like you, I believe strongly in widening the net, so consider being a little broad-minded in your selection of your competitors. I also believe you can learn from every retailer, not just from your direct competition. A good idea, even from a retailer in a different business, can often be adapted to fit yours.

Your mission in shopping the competition is to learn as much as you can about what your competitors are doing that can affect your business, help clarify your mission, and ultimately improve your business. Specifically, you want to identify any strength you might incorporate into your operation, and you want to learn any weaknesses that you might take advantage of.

That sounds so simple, but it takes discipline and preparation to get the most from a competitive visit, and it takes a mind-set of learning. All too often I have seen young buyers who simply spend the morning competitive shopping with no preparation, no notes, and no results because they really only went to prove to themselves that their operation was better. The objective is not to prove who is better—the objective is to learn what will make your operation better and improve your competitive edge.

Finally, you must keep aware of the competitive landscape because it is always changing, and to be successful you often have to change with it. Even the most successful stores usually need to reinvent themselves eventually to stay ahead of the pack and keep their leading edge.

Preparing for a Visit to a Competitor

Let me begin by stressing that there is nothing illegal or immoral about shopping the competition. Indeed it is one of the very best tools a retailer, especially an independent, has for learning and garnering information to help his or her business become more profitable.

Most shopkeepers do not like competitive shoppers because, of course, store owners want to keep their state secrets to themselves. Some will even ask you to leave if they determine that you are a competitor. While there are some retail experts who suggest going about competitive shopping quite openly, in my many years of shopping my competitors I have not found that to be the best approach. It is often the best way to be shown the door, but I believe it is seldom the best approach to really learn about your competitor's operation.

Instead, I think there are two approaches that are far more successful. You can hire a shopping service whose personnel know just how to go about it and are not, of course, from your store. But I believe the far better way is for you to go yourself, armed with a plausible story, a disguise if you will, about why you are shopping your designated retailer. As a female buyer I was in great demand to play wife when one of my male counterparts wanted to go competitive shopping; and in return I always made "my husband" go competitive shopping with me as repayment for my shopping service. Also, a little rehearsal as to what you are shopping for goes a long way toward making your shopping expedition convincing and more fruitful.

Make some notes before you go about what you want to learn, and be sure to take a notebook, or make things even easier and use a small voice recorder to keep track of your observations and details on pricing and the like so that you can evaluate better after you leave the store. I developed a little form with a list of questions that I would take with me and answer after I left the store while everything was still fresh in my mind. This checklist would often make me go back into the store to check something I had completely overlooked but was important enough to be on my list.

The more you know about your competitor, the more meaningful your trip will be. You will observe more, and you will have a better idea of what to concentrate on.

Ways to Learn about Your Competitors

Reading Competitors' Ads. As a background to a competitive visit, be sure you have read the company's ads and visited its website, if there is one. Competitors' ads will reveal a great deal about their operations. By following them over a period of time you will be able to tell without even entering the store what their best categories and their best items are. Their ads are educating not only the customer but you too. Their pricing strategy and price lines will also become apparent, as will many of the key points in their customer-service policies.

Your Vendors. They can be a wealth of information about your competitors, especially if they sell to them as well. Often they will be only too happy to show off by telling you how much they know about your competitors. Sometimes this information has to be taken with a grain of salt, but often some very interesting and actionable information will surface if you ask just a few questions of the right people.

Your Customers. Ask them which other stores they shop for your kind of merchandise and why. You may be surprised at some of the insights your customers may have into the competition and what keys to success these may hold for you.

People You Know. Talk about your business and your competitors with your friends and associates. They are all customers, too, and quite often you will be amazed by how poignant an observation can come from someone who is not in your business at all.

Things to Check Out on Competitive Visits

Target Audience. Who are their customers? How do they reach them to bring them into their stores?

Location and Size. Where are they located, and how big are they? Do these factors give them some sort of special advantage?

Windows (If Any). How appealing are they? Do they make you want to go inside? How effective are they at communicating the store's mission?

Communication of Mission. Upon entering the store, how readily do you get its mission? How compelling is it? Does the store reflect what the windows promise?

Overall Appearance. In general, how appealing is the store? How is the housekeeping? How comfortable does the store make you feel? How well are the store and the merchandise signed?

Layout, Fixturing, and Ambience. How does the layout compare to yours? How is the customer led through the store? Is there something special to be learned here regarding the fixturing? How are the lighting, the music selection, and the ambience in general?

Displays. Do they tell stories well? Do they use cross-merchandising effectively? Do the displays support the mission of the store?

Merchandise. Identify the following:
- main merchandise categories
- strengths and weaknesses
- the quality and value offered
- price ranges and pricing philosophy
- uniqueness versus basics
- freshness and cleanliness
- general competitiveness
- anything especially noteworthy

Customer Service. Evaluate these elements:
- the number and the quality of the sales staff
- the employees' appearance, product knowledge, and competency
- the effectiveness of price tickets and signage, including product information
- notification of store policies (Are all store policies clearly signed?)
- methods of payment

- delivery service
- hours of operation
- ease of checkout
- gift wrap availability and cost
- hours of operation
- special practices or value-added services

Purchases. What are people buying, or what categories are they primarily shopping?

Traffic. How does it compare to yours at a comparable time, and what does that indicate about the size of your competitors' businesses as compared to yours?

Evaluating Your Shopping Experience

Three Key Questions to Ask Yourself about Your Competitor. When you review your observations about your competitor, you should ask yourself the following questions:

- What are the things that they are doing well that I can either copy or reinterpret for my store?
- What are they doing so well that I should not spend too much effort trying to copy it? (For example, they may have a category, minor to your vision, that they have exploded and really own.)
- What are the categories or things they are not doing well that I can capitalize on in my store?

Actions. There are a number of specific action areas that usually result from a competitive shopping experience, any number of which you may decide to apply to your operation.

- **Increase, decrease, or eliminate categories or products.** For example, adding a new line or item;

stocking unusual sizes or items; or offering special-order items/sizes to get the same effect.

- **Raise or lower prices on selected items.** You might do this where you can either make more margin dollars or become more competitive.
- **Increase or refocus your advertising or promotional events.** In particular, this should play to your strengths and tell your story.
- **Refine customer-service issues.** This could include staffing, customer guarantees, store hours, store signage concepts, or expanding value-added services.
- **Adapt display techniques.** Changing elements like fixtures or other aspects of store design could spruce up your store.

Remember, if you come away with just one good idea, your trip has been worthwhile—and chances are, you will certainly find more than one. So formulize your thoughts into an action plan and go for it!

CHAPTER 7

Differentiating Your Product Line

In addition to making your store unique with your ambience, categories/classifications, customer service, and value-added services, the main key, of course, is the merchandise you carry. Of all the elements that make a store successful, none is as critical as the merchandise you sell. Therefore, differentiating your assortment from those of your competitors is perhaps the largest weapon in your retailing arsenal. There are many ways to accomplish this. One of the most effective ways to set your store apart is to be aware of the current trends, and to utilize and capitalize on the ones that will enhance your product line and store.

Understanding Trends and Their Application

Deciding How Trendy You Want to Be. This must be your first decision. Barney's, for example, always wants to be on the cutting edge, often in fact creating the trends, whereas Macy's for many years wanted to be on the trend when it was cresting—not too soon and not after it was post peak. Some stores that are primarily price driven are comfortable with merchandise exhibiting trends that are post peak, or even at the bottom of the trend curve.

Merriam-Webster's Eleventh Collegiate Dictionary defines *trend* as "a prevailing tendency; a current style or preference." Trends have longer life cycles, making them quite different from fads, which Webster's describes as "a practice or interest followed for a time with exaggerated zeal." Fads come quickly and go just as quickly, and they usually affect only one group of people rather than the multitudes. The pet rock is a good example of a fad, while natural products are a current trend.

Retailers are looking to capitalize on both trends and fads, and often use the terms interchangeably. However, fads, which can mean quick business overnight, and often lots of it, can also disappear almost as quickly, leaving enormous markdowns behind, so they should be monitored carefully. Fads are easy to spot because they become so obvious so quickly and often seem to be everywhere in the media. Trends, on the other hand, come on more slowly and can last years, decades, or even centuries. The rewards for finding trends and capitalizing on them can also be large, and they have the added advantage of lasting longer and dying more slowly, usually making them safer investments.

The Trend Curve. This is a life cycle similar to that which most living things follow. There is a beginning, a maturity, and an ending. Different types of retailers are usually found concentrating on different parts of the curve. Emerging trends are seen by fewer customers in boutiques and specialty stores, usually at higher price points. Upward trends are more broadly exposed, normally to consumers in better department stores. Peak trends are also seen in department stores, and they are available to a broad consumer base at popular prices. Post peak is available at a broader range of stores, including department and midtier retailers. Bottom of the curve is the broadest level, available at all price points, affordable to everyone, and seen at mass merchants, drugstores, and the like.

Where to Look for Trends. Today's trends are literally all around you. A trend will start slowly and be in evidence in a few places, but as it grows it will become more obvious until it is seen in many different places. In addition to observing those in the various retailers, there are plenty of other places to get a fix on what is happening today. The most obvious is the media, since their job is primarily reporting what is new. Some of the best are as follows:

Newspapers. Many people naturally think first of the *New York Times,* but there are others that are well worth reading as well. *USA Today* has a snapshot section on the front page and articles that focus on lifestyle events. *USA Today's* trends appeal to the mass population and are at the upward point on the trend curve. The *Wall Street Journal* focuses on advance trends, at the beginning of the trend curve, and appeals to consumers in higher economic strata.

Magazines. As an example, those catering to home furnishings— *Elle Décor, Martha Stewart Living, Traditional Home,* and *Marie Claire,* to name just a few—cover both foreign and domestic trends. Some of the home/shelter magazines (*Elle Décor* and *House Beautiful*) usually have a collage near the beginning of the magazine identifying the trends they see six months or so before they are really evident in the marketplace. Other businesses have similar magazines aimed at those businesses, so hunt down the ones that cater to yours.

Trade Journals. Almost all trade journals report the trends in their business as one of their most important features. However, most often these trends are being reported as they are evident in the market, not usually months in advance as in the better shelter magazines.

Trend Services. These are for those most serious about trends, those whom we call trend masters. They not only spot trends but also create products from those trends; in contrast, trend spotters use the trends to guide their merchandise purchases. Trend services typically forecast out a year or two. They are used to inspire and help create new ideas and visions. They also tend to be pricey for an independent business. However, trend services frequently lecture at trade shows (like the Cotton Inc. show), where you can learn from them—usually for free or as part of the entrance fee to a trade show (trade shows are discussed in greater detail below).

Museum Exhibits, TV Programs, Movies, and Plays. These and other forms of entertainment are a mirror of what is happening in our society. A good example was the TV series *Sex and the City* (and the movies based on it), in which Sarah Jessica Parker's clothes, shoes, and hats were definitely on-trend or fashion-forward.

Websites. There are lots of free websites for which you can sign up that will give you daily or weekly updates.

HFNmag.com (http://www.hfnmag.com) reports news from the trade magazine *HFN*, covering the home industry with frequent trend reporting.

DailyCandy (http://www.dailycandy.com) offers "a hand-picked selection of all that is fun, fashionable, food related, and culturally stimulating in the city you're fixated on (and all over the Web)."[29]

The website for the cotton industry (http://www.cottoninc.com) relates all sorts of news and happenings, but it also has excellent trend reports for both ready-to-wear (RTW) and home goods.

Trendwatching.com (http://www.trendwatching.com) offers a free trend service: "One of the world's leading trend firms, trendwatching.com scans the globe for emerging consumer trends. We report on our findings in free, monthly Trend Briefings which get sent to 160,000 subscribers … To make sure you never miss a

---

29   "Welcome to DailyCandy," *DailyCandy*, http://www.dailycandy.com/all-cities/ (accessed April 6, 2012).

briefing again, just enter your e-mail address and we'll notify you when new editions become available."[30]

The Pantone site (http://www.pantone.com) allows you to sign up for free to get color trend information from Pantone's trend service. Pantone Colors are a universal numerical system used by professionals in print, as well as in ready-to-wear, men's fashions, and home furnishings. Pantone Inc., which sets the trends for color, issues its new forecasted colors for the next season, usually in conjunction with the major seasonal trade shows, and makes them available then on the Pantone website.

There are various other news websites that often report on trends, including www.time.com, www.crainsnewyork.com, and www.newyorktimes.com.

Trade Shows. These shows of course are excellent venues for spotting and monitoring trends in your business. Most of the important manufacturers show, and most of their management-level employees, who are usually only too happy to discuss their take on the trends in their business, usually attend. Obviously, trade shows in the United States are easier to attend, but you could consider combining a vacation with the timing of a foreign trade show.

Almost every major retail business has a trade show for the purpose of presenting its vendors' wares to the buyers. Cities like New York host a great many of them. New York, Chicago, Los Angeles, and Atlanta, all of which have regional shows, may be good starting points; but each industry has its "show of shows" where the most important new trends and merchandise are showcased.

Some of the more noteworthy domestic shows for trend spotting in home furnishings are as follows:

- Atlanta Mart (and Gift Show) for giftware and home furnishings
- Las Vegas Mart for gifts, furniture, and textiles

30 "About trendwatching.com," *trendwatching.com,* http://www.trend watching.com/ (accessed April 16, 2012).

- New York Stationery Show
- New York Gift Show
- Fancy Food Show (NASFT), which changes location every year
- High Point Furniture Show for furniture, lamps, and accessories

The most noteworthy overseas are:

- Maison Object (http://www.maison-object.com)
- Ambiente (http://www.ambiente.messefrankfurt.com)

Your vendors, either current ones or those from whom you intend to buy in the future, will be able to advise you on the important trade shows for your business.

How to Spot Trends. It is easy enough if you are reading or viewing any of the resources mentioned previously that are highlighting the trends for you, but what if you want to identify them yourself? Spotting trends is not, as some imagine, looking into a crystal ball; nor are trends only obvious to a select few. Anyone can spot trends because, as we have said, they are all around you. To be really proficient at spotting them, you have to observe. You have to be curious and open-minded, and want to look for them; and you must look for them across industry lines. You also have to note those you see, catalog them, and analyze your observations to distill them down into the trends you might want to use.

If you want to be on the forefront, traveling helps because some places are much richer in exhibiting coming trends than others. For example, in the United States the three top cities where trends become apparent first are New York, San Francisco, and Los Angeles.

Let's talk about one of the most basic and common ways for retailers to identify trends that are directly relevant to their business: identifying trends at a trade show. I have already noted that one way is to talk to your key vendors and ask them what they are seeing. This is a good source because, as important vendors of yours, their position on trends and the trend curve will most likely mirror your own.

But how else can you shop the show to identify new trends that may be important for your business? I suggest that you set aside three hours to walk the show just to look for trends, focusing particularly on the most fashion-forward vendors. (Do not be tempted to stop along the way to do business, because you will lose your concentration!)

You are looking for repetition of a color, detail, or new item. Whatever these vendors are showing in the front of their spaces is what they consider to be the newest fashion statement for them. Start noting anything that particularly catches your eye in a small notebook or electronic device, or by taking a picture (if you are permitted). Take note the second time you see it and the third and the fourth ... by then you probably have a trend. (You may have to backtrack if you see something and remember that you saw it earlier.)

Gathering information or noting repetition of detail or color is the principle by which you can identify trends in any medium, whether in a newspaper, magazine, or elsewhere. It is noting that small detail that reoccurs and reoccurs that leads you to identify the new trends.

How to Use Your Trends. First, it should be noted that as an independent you have an advantage over the larger retailers in capitalizing on trends, because with your smaller size you are more flexible and can move faster than the big guys, which is the reason why so many retail trends are spotted first in upper-end specialty stores.

After you have decided on the trends you want to develop/express in your store, it is time to put them down on paper or in your electronic mobile device so you can take them to market and not forget some of the details. This will also enable you to explain them to someone else, such as a vendor from whom you might be looking for some of the merchandise to fit into your trend, or employees who need to know. When, and if, you are big enough, you may even be asking your vendors to create merchandise for you to fit into your trends, in which case you will need something to leave with your supplier.

Each trend should have a theme, some key elements to use in it, and a color palette so that it will all coordinate and hang together as a cohesive whole. In a small store, two or three trends for a major season are enough. Furthermore, the colors of the different themes are better if they are compatible, rather than in conflict with each other, because this will allow greater freedom of movement of the themes around the store and a better overall visual effect.

To illustrate this point, let us pretend you own a gift store and you have picked two themes for Christmas: snowmen and Santa Claus. These may well be the same two themes you had last year, since there are only a finite number of appropriate themes. However, last year your snowman was quite childlike and the Santa was more Old World. For this year you have decided on a more contemporary Santa theme and a more sophisticated, whimsical snowman.

For the snowman theme, you have chosen to use snowflakes as an important element, while candy canes will be a main element for your Santa theme. When you established your Pantone colors for the two themes this year, you changed last year's traditional Christmas green to the newer citrus green in the Santa theme, and you will add lots of a vivid blue to this year's snowman theme.

You have found a product line of ceramics featuring a Santa for your Santa theme, and one for the snowman theme, to build your stories around. As you build your theme, you will search out and add different coordinating items, consistent in detail and color palette, until the story comes alive.

With the basics of the themes decided, many merchants will prepare a trend board for each theme using a foam-core board, fleshing the theme out with clippings from catalogs and magazines, adding swatches, and even hanging merchandise on the board to give the flavor. The board is completed by adding the Pantone colors to it.

At this point in the process you would take a picture and gather your Pantone chips, and you would have a blueprint to take shopping at market. Others do their blueprints as PowerPoint presentations, running off extra copies to take to market to keep on course and to use with their vendors. Still others will simply take a notebook and put a couple of representative pictures, some buzzwords, and their Pantone chips in it as their aid for market. (Pantone colors, as I mentioned previously, are a universal numerical system used by professionals in print, ready-to-wear, and home furnishings.)

Whichever method you choose, you do need some sort of pictorial reminder and some color swatches to ensure that your themes come out as you envision them. It would be impossible for most people to remember all the details accurately and to describe them, or the colors, to a vendor. I suggest using Pantone colors, as they are almost universally recognized.

Finding and Developing Unique Items

Exclusives. Perhaps the most common and widely used method of differentiating a retailer's product line from those of his competitors is to negotiate exclusives from his or her suppliers. The big guys usually work with their suppliers well in advance of the buying season, and before the major trade shows, to review their vendors' upcoming products, select the ones that they want (either as part of their trend statements or basic merchandise offering), and "tie the item(s) up" for their market. Usually, but not always, this requires a substantial commitment to the vendor. The exclusive may be ongoing, or it may just be to break the item into their markets and have it exclusively for a specified period of time.

Develop Merchandise with Suppliers. In addition to negotiating for items on an exclusive basis, many of the larger retailers work with select vendors to develop merchandise especially for them. These might be items to fit into their most current trends (as we have previously described) or simply good basic merchandise for which they have a void in their assortment. Since the retailer has collaborated in the development of the item, it will normally be guaranteed as an exclusive for the life of the product but will often also carry a hefty commitment with it.

With their greater buying power, larger retailers obviously have a much easier time than independents in developing a range of unique merchandise to differentiate their stores by obtaining exclusives or having vendors create merchandise especially for them. However, depending on the commodity, this is by no means impossible for the smaller retailer.

Utilize Special Types of Vendors. This will enable you to find and present merchandise that is different from that of your competitors, especially your large ones.

Craftspeople, no matter what your type of merchandise, are likely to be making items by hand that could fit into your operation and add a touch of exclusivity to your store. Your store could be a great venue for selling a craftsperson's wares, because you probably can't use more than the craftsperson can produce. Most craftspeople cannot approach the larger stores, because they couldn't produce enough for them, and since they are making them by hand, their wares will be more expensive than machine-made products in the same category, but they may be perfect for your operation. Often craftspeople will come to you, having identified your store as one that might sell their items.

Boutique vendors specialize in selling to smaller retailers. These suppliers understand your need for exclusivity and merchandise that will set you apart in the marketplace and will work with you to help you achieve this. More often than not they are more upscale vendors, which is an added advantage for this more unique merchandise.

Jobbers can help you to create a little excitement. You should develop relationships with some closeout vendors or jobbers who from time to time have the kind of merchandise you sell, often in smaller quantities that can be appropriate only for a smaller retailer. This type of merchandise can serve the dual purpose of exclusivity and will often let you offer some very good sales with little or no markdown liability.

Importers are also an avenue where you may find some unusual merchandise not found everywhere. The caution here is that they may be selling items similar to those the big guys are importing on their own at more advantageous pricing, so you do have to be careful.

Create Your Own Gift Sets. Many retail shops sell merchandise that can be packaged together to make a unique gift. As was already mentioned, the best example I know in the home business is Williams-Sonoma, which packages its food with cookbooks or cooking items to create attractive and unique gifts. And if you don't like the ones they have made, you can just pick your own stuff, and they will create a wonderful gift confection tailor-made for you.

A friend of mine who owns a small gift shop does the same thing, using wonderful ribbons and cello wrap to let the merchandise show through. Not only do these ready-made gifts go like hot cakes for various gift-giving occasions, but when mixed throughout the merchandise displays, they add a wonderful unique flair to the whole store.

Private-Label Merchandise. These products are an excellent way of adding individuality to your store. Many items can be made yours by having them packaged with your store's name on the label. Supermarkets are famous for their own brand merchandise, which is usually nothing more than a manufacturer's item packaged with the retailer's name on it. Gift shops in particular often have a field day with this—selling all manner of things like soaps, perfumes, and even candy under their name. Although the minimums are often high, whenever it is affordable, this is an excellent way of adding prestige and uniqueness or, depending on how you price it, a value image to your store.

Along these lines, as was previously mentioned, a method that is very effective (and usually affordable) in enhancing your image is developing your own gift boxes, ribbons, and gift cards with your logo or store name. These can usually be hot-stamped and, depending upon how much you want to spend, can be tailor-made to your image by any number of suppliers and add an aura of class to any gifts you sell.

In addition to having your own gift wrap, embossed seals can be made for your store to use on packages, which add a bit of class and distinction to the gift as well.

All of the above can be effective in helping you differentiate your store and express your store's mission. Using these resources, you can make your store be as individual as you want it to be. Funding aside, you will be limited only by your own imagination.

I am reminded of what my college guidance counselor said to me all those years ago when I told her I planned to go into retailing: "Stores are like people; find the one that you like, and you will be very successful." She was right. Your store is like a person. You can give her or him whatever personality you want; and, in my opinion, this is the most fun part of retailing.

CHAPTER 8

Utilizing Vendors More Effectively

Your merchandise is as good as your stable of suppliers, who can also be very helpful partners in building your profitability if you utilize them effectively. One of the easiest ways to keep your assortment fresh and timely is to continually find and add new suppliers who bring fresh ideas and merchandise to your store, while replacing older ones whose wares are not selling as well as they used to. Whether you are looking for trends, exclusives, or just saleable merchandise, there are any number of ways to find new suppliers and elicit their help. But first, it is helpful to understand the distribution channels for your business (some of which I described in chapter 7) and their various strengths and weaknesses. Although there are several ways of categorizing them, and the lines between them are often blurred, I will try to keep it simple.

Types of Suppliers

Manufacturers. These companies design and manufacture the product; they may sell directly to retailers through their own sales force, or they may have distributors or agents who in turn sell to the retailer. An example is Simmons Mattress Company (for whom I worked), which manufactured the totality of its products from raw materials it bought from others and which had its own dedicated sales force that sold to the retailer.

If the manufacturer sells directly through its sales force, this is usually the cheapest way to procure the goods. The caution here is that the minimum orders are sometimes high—and the freight for such large orders may also be high.

Marketer/Manufacturers. While they act like manufacturers in that they design the line and sell it to retailers, marketer/manufacturers mainly create a brand and subcontract the products from other manufacturers. I worked for Dansk International, basically a marketer, which subcontracted most of its wares from factories all over the world.

Both sell their products in the same way. They often attend major trade shows and have a website that gives pertinent information, such as how to contact them, facts about their wares, and so on. Many have permanent showrooms, as well as their own salespeople or independent salespeople (known as manufacturer's representatives), who call on customers and sell their products.

Distributors and Wholesalers. These suppliers buy from the foreign or domestic manufacturer, usually in large quantities, and resell the products to retailers in smaller quantities. To be technical, distributors generally represent a factory (usually one) and carry a large inventory of their wares, while a wholesaler usually sells several factories' merchandise directly to the retailer; but they both service the retailer in pretty much the same way.

Many wholesalers have elaborate showrooms in which they showcase their lines. The advantage here is that these vendors normally have multiple lines that are usually compatible, so the retailer can often write a single order for several different items or lines and can often consolidate all the items into one shipment to save on the freight that multiple shipments would cost.

Also, it is often possible to build special relationships with these vendors, and, as you become more important to them, you may be able to get additional concessions, like exclusivity or the ability to be first in your market with a new item. The smart distributors and wholesalers will often work a market so that competitors do not have the same merchandise.

Jobbers. These suppliers usually specialize in closeouts and can be useful in adding some promotional spice to your business. They will often seek out smaller retailers because their quantities may be too small for the big guys, who will often buy these closeouts directly from the manufacturer. In some industries jobbers perform another function. They often rent a space in an existing store and provide all the merchandising functions for their goods in that space.

Importers. These vendors buy and sell foreign goods. They can be a valuable resource in helping differentiate your business, since they usually offer goods that are unique and often less expensive than American-made ones.

Craftspeople. These suppliers produce their own product and can become, as was previously mentioned, an important element in creating your strategic message by adding an air of exclusivity to your assortment.

Where to Find Suppliers

Finding suppliers is easy, and there are many avenues to locate them—but tracking down the ones that have just what you want takes an ongoing effort. Some of the best ways are discussed below:

Your Store. When you have a store, suppliers will often find you. Usually smaller independents will see salespeople when they come to their store with or without an appointment. As you grow bigger and more vendors want to see you, you might want to establish a vendor day—one day of the week when you see vendors in the morning or afternoon. This way you will not miss them when you are out of the store, and they will appreciate not missing you on a visit when they make a sales call when you are not in.

Competitors. Another way to find new suppliers is by visiting your competitors' stores and searching for items that would fit into your store. If the product is massed out, usually their boxes, from which you can determine the manufacturer, are visible too. By contacting the manufacturer you can learn how, or from whom, you can purchase this product.

Trade Shows. One of the best ways to find suppliers is to attend trade shows for the kind of merchandise that you sell and walk aisle by aisle looking for vendors who sell merchandise you can envision in your store. As you find them, be sure to take all of their contact information and ask about the clientele they sell. That will tell you as much as anything if they will be suitable for your operation. Birds of a feather flock together, right?

Trade Publications. Most trade publications (like *HFN* for home furnishings) will review the major vendors prior to a trade show, write a review on them, and showcase the items they think are the most trendy or noteworthy. This is a great resource for finding new suppliers that might meet your needs. In addition, most of the trade papers will also carry vendor ads, which will give you a flavor of what these vendors think is the most important in their line for the upcoming season and will give you a clue about if they are worth a visit.

Trade Organizations. If your business has a trade organization, joining it should give you access to all the most important suppliers, as well as a good deal of information about them.

Buying Groups. Joining these associations of retailers, who have formed an association to get better deals from manufacturers, is another good way to find vendors that can meet your needs. The furniture business is particularly replete with these types of associations. While there is normally a fee to join them, there are usually counterbalancing savings to be had in better pricing from vendors, and lots of valuable information to be gleaned through networking with the various members.

Buying Services. All kinds are available to retailers as they grow in size, from trend services to merchandise offers to, perhaps the most popular, foreign buying services for sourcing abroad.

Craft Shows. As was mentioned earlier, many of these craftspeople will come to your store, but a good place to find them is at the various craft shows in your locale and around the country.

Other Vendors. When you find vendors that you like, ask what other vendors they consider to be their competition. Chances are the ones they name will be quite similar to your vendor and would probably be worth a look.

The Web. As for everything else we search for these days, with a little effort you can find appropriate vendors on the web. There are many resources listing various sources for all kinds of products and businesses, and you can also use your search engine for the business you are researching.

Suppliers as Consultants

Finding good suppliers is only half the battle. How can you use them to your best advantage? I have known many retailers who consider their suppliers enemies rather than partners in their business. They have a "we versus them" attitude and as such miss out on one of the biggest benefits you can get from your suppliers.

The truth is that suppliers can be your biggest partners in increasing your profitability.

Let Your Vendors Educate You. While there are many things you can get from a vendor in addition to merchandise, I have often felt one of the most important is knowledge and insights into the business. They can be a tremendous source of useful information. Most suppliers, especially manufacturers, know a huge amount about their businesses. Each owner has probably lived it 24/7 for years and years and has forgotten more about it than you may even care to know. Suppliers generally love their business and, if asked questions, will give like a fountain.

Many young buyers are often reluctant to ask their vendors questions, because they feel it shows they don't know something. To the contrary, this often forms a bond with suppliers, who are all too anxious to share their knowledge in hopes that it might help sell their product better. One of the hardest things I had to teach my buyers was to ask what the new trends were and what items from this supplier were the hottest. If a supplier's line is right for your store, chances are very good that his or her newer trends will become yours, and his or her best sellers could be yours as well.

Furthermore, too many young buyers have pride of authorship and want to buy what they like rather than what will most likely sell. I have found that setting aside personal tastes is one of the hardest lessons of all to learn in retailing, but learning what the best sellers are can really pay off.

Evaluate Your Vendors

Suppliers are a little like your friends. They have different personalities, as well as different strengths and weaknesses, and each brings something different to the party. Obviously having a solid vendor roster is extremely desirable, but in order to develop one you have to, above all, be objective. Unlike your friends, you may not even like some of your suppliers, but because of their product lines or other considerations, they may be among your most valuable ones. Maximizing your vendor opportunities also requires an ongoing evaluation of them.

Start the process by asking yourself who your biggest vendor is and why. Is it because of the product, the pricing, the service, or all of the above? Chances are it is all.

The Most Important Criteria. They are the product, its appeal to your customer, and pricing. As has been said before, the pricing doesn't have to be the cheapest, but it does have to be fair in relationship to the product and its competition. Merchandise that turns often, sells quickly at a fair markup, and doesn't sit on your shelves to be marked down is the stuff from which profit is made. It follows, therefore, that vendors who supply the most merchandise of this ilk are those to be cultivated and grown, no matter what you think of their egos or personalities.

Other Factors. There are many other important considerations to think of, many of which fall under the umbrella of service, when evaluating the worth of your suppliers:

Availability of the product is often not afforded its real importance, but it is vitally important. To be able to get a constant replenishment of your best sellers is critical to maximizing them and your business.

Complete and on-time deliveries are also critical. One thing I have learned over the years is to ask for and to be realistic about the lead time a supplier needs. Young buyers for large companies often feel that since they have "a large pencil," they will get preferential treatment, so they need not be concerned with the supplier's normal lead time. Wrong! What they fail to realize is that when Bloomingdale's is yelling for shipment of a product, so is Macy's and probably some other large retailer as well.

Consistency and quality must be evaluated as well. A defective piece of merchandise can do more than anything else, except perhaps poor customer service, to turn a customer off to your store.

Product-support materials—for example, fliers or other printed information on the products you carry from them—are silent salesmen that help the product move faster.

Brand-name recognition also works in suppliers' favor. Does the product have a brand name that enhances your customer's view of your store? For its quality? Its fashion-forwardness? While it is hard to put an exact price on this, this definitely provides added value to your vendor's worth.

Special terms, allowances, and concessions take a myriad of different forms in the marketplace, which you must be aware of when you are doing business and must consider when you are evaluating your vendors. I will discuss these in depth in the next section.

These elements should be considered when looking at the true profitability of your vendors. Add them all up, and you may be surprised as to just which of your vendors is the most profitable and therefore should be considered the most valuable to your business.

Vendor Report Card. Some retailers I know have established a report card for their vendors, listing the key areas (above) to rate, and a point system from 1 to 5, with 5 being best. All the items are tallied by vendor, and the vendors with the highest totals become their preferred vendors. While this takes some discipline, it is a worthwhile endeavor to undertake once a year to determine which vendors you want to emphasize in the coming year. It also serves as a reminder about vendors who need to improve in certain areas to warrant more of your business, which you can discuss with them at your next meeting.

Concessions to Increase Your Profitability

Perhaps the most obvious things to ask for are a better price, exclusivity on an item, or the ability to break the item first in a market—all of which I have previously discussed—but there are a myriad of other factors that can bring substantial extra profits.

Discounts. There are many kinds of discounts, but the most prevalent are discussed below:

Cash discounts consist of two parts: the discount percent, which will be deducted from the invoice if the payment is made on time, and the dating, the number of days within which payment must be made in order to get the discount. Dating generally begins on the day the merchandise and the invoice are received. Ordinary dating of 2%/10 days, for example, means that 2 percent can be deducted from the invoice if it is paid within ten days from the receipt of the merchandise and invoice.

Extra dating is additional payment time granted by the vendor. Obviously, the longer the better. An example of extra dating is the early-buy discount, when a vendor offers an extra discount for placing your order early and receiving the goods in advance of the selling season. Examples of industries where extra dating is commonplace are the Trim-A-Home world and summer furniture. In some industries like these, months-long payment terms are the norm.

Quantity discounts are graduating discounts based on the quantity purchased. Most vendors have such discounts and they are enticing, but beware of falling into the trap of buying more than you need just to get the discount. This is indeed penny-wise and pound-foolish.

Cumulative quantity discounts increase with the cumulative amount of the item purchased by the buyer, usually within a specified period of time.

Opening-order discounts are given for the beginning of a new program to help offset future markdowns.

New-store discounts are sometimes given to buyers opening new stores as a token of assistance for the expense of the new store.

Promotional discounts are offered for a short period of time in order to stimulate the sales of a product.

Other special discounts may be offered by vendors (usually to the big guys) in lieu of receiving any charge-backs for damaged or defective goods.

Allowances. In addition to discounts, many suppliers also offer various types of allowances that can again be used to increase your profits.

The advertising allowance, perhaps the most common, can often be negotiated if you plan to advertise the product. While this is a major point of negotiations for the big guys, you should ask for it too. It is, after all, to the vendor's benefit also to help you sell more of his or her merchandise. Usually reimbursement will require proof of advertising, but that is usually well worth the trouble to receive extra funds to stimulate the sales of the product.

The display allowance is a rarer cousin of the advertising allowance, in which the supplier will pay for special displays of his or her product, like featuring the item in your window.

Guaranteed sale is another allowance that is sometimes available. It is, as the name implies, an agreement with the vendor that if the merchandise does not sell after a certain length of time, it can be returned to him or her for credit or a refund. The one caution here is to be sure the merchandise will probably sell in your store. Otherwise you may fall into the trap of using valuable floor space that could be better utilized by other merchandise to take advantage of this guarantee.

Prepaid freight or partially paid freight is when a vendor will share in the expense of getting the merchandise to you. Or if you are near the vendor's warehouse or factory, the company may let you come and pick up the goods, which can also be a real money saver.

Markdown money/returns help when you are stuck with some merchandise that just won't sell. Ask your vendor what he or she can do to help you. Perhaps the vendor can take it back in exchange for new merchandise, or give you markdown money. Remember, it is to the vendor's advantage for you to clear the slow-moving product, because it is taking up space that some of his or her more salable goods might occupy.

Rebate programs are usually most applicable to larger retailers. However, many vendors offer rebate programs (a cash incentive) with an ever-increasing percentage of rebate when certain volume levels are reached.

Other Concessions. Many other goodies are sometimes available from your vendors:

Off-price or closeout merchandise, inventory that a manufacturer or importer has marked down to clear it, are products you might be able to sell at full retail for extra markup or at a sharp sale price at your regular markup for extra volume. You have to ask aggressively for these goods because they usually carry a smaller commission, so your salespeople will probably prefer to sell you regular goods. Also, if it is an attractive closeout, it is usually reserved for, and offered first to, the most important customers.

Promotional merchandise, goods that the supplier has produced or purchased to be sold at a reduced price, can allow you to offer your customers a sharp deal without shortening your markup.

Free fixturing is something Christmas-card vendors will usually do, or vendors will help defray the expense of props or fixtures for their merchandise.

Demos conducted in your store by a representative from your supplier (the rep comes to your store and demonstrates how to use the products you are selling) create extra interest in the products.

Trunk shows can take the form of additional merchandise on consignment, often coupled with a representative from the company who has catalogs or photos of other items in the line that can be special-ordered for your customer. This is an especially fine way of reaching out to specific customers and showing expertise in a category.

Merchandise on consignment are goods that some suppliers will let you offer for sale without paying for them until they are sold, or you may return them to the supplier after a specified time if they have not been sold. But beware, like guaranteed sale, this can be a trap. As attractive as this sounds, be sure it is the right merchandise for your store. Otherwise it will just take up valuable space that a better-selling line might occupy.

Other Vendor Services. There are other things that vendors can do for you:

- Count their goods and help write reorders.
- Hold sales meetings about their products and often provide coffee and donuts for your salespeople.
- Pre-ticket their merchandise for you (usually for a small charge), if you are big enough.

There are undoubtedly others I have forgotten, but this should serve as a pretty good checklist.

With all these goodies available for which the retailer may negotiate, it is most important to note that many independents do not even consider asking for many of these things, because they believe they are too small to qualify for them.

Let me tell you a story that taught me quite lesson in this regard many years ago when I was a VP at Macy's. Pricing matters were somewhat flexible then, and I headed up the home division in Macy's corporate buying division, which had the mission of getting the six Macy's divisions located across the United States to harness their buying power to purchase goods together. In this process, to make a corporate purchase or contract, we would target a key item or line that was suitable for all divisions. Then, to begin the negotiation at the lowest price, we would canvas the divisions to find out what each division was currently paying for the item (although it might have been expected that they would all have been the same). Otherwise, one would naturally think that the powerful Macy's New York, or the young aggressive upstart Bamberger's, or the very chic Macy's California was paying the lowest price. However, more often than not, it would be the little LaSalle and Koch division in Toledo, Ohio—which was so small their branch stores were called twigs.

Why, you might ask, did the smallest division get the lowest price? Sometimes the vendors felt sorry for them because they were overshadowed by the other, much larger divisions, but more often, since a very low price on a small order cost the vendor practically nothing, he could easily afford to be a hero with LaSalle and Koch. In addition, most of their buyers were very seasoned professionals who were masters at working their vendors and getting all that they legally could.

Please think about this story. Whatever you ask for will cost the vendor a fraction of what it would cost them to offer the same benefit to a larger retailer. Don't be timid. You may never know the lowest price available or whatever other concessions may be available to you if you don't ask.

Over the years I have found that many retailers are afraid to ask for these extra goodies because they are afraid to be turned down and will take it personally if they are. But the truth is you are not being rejected; this is just a matter of business. Furthermore, while you will probably get more than you expected, the most they can say is no, but they will respect you for trying.

If you don't ask, you probably won't get—and you certainly won't get as much as if you asked. Remember, a good part of the retailing game is negotiating, which can also be one of the most fun and rewarding parts.

Finally, as a note of caution, the customs and laws regarding legalities in buying and selling are, like most other areas, somewhat flexible and do change, so it is wise to find a retail lawyer who can keep you up to date and offer clarification if you are in doubt.

CHAPTER 9

Refining Your Store and Product Line

You have undoubtedly heard many times that a sale begins with consumers' wants or needs. These are often talked about interchangeably, and while there may sometimes be a thin line dividing the two, they are really quite different. A need is something one has to have, like food. A want is something one desires but can do without, like a hot fudge sundae. Clearly, if you are supplying needs, you have an easier time of making a sale. Yet almost all retailers prosper on delivering what the customer wants.

When customers come to your store, they start with some very broad and basic wants.

General Guidelines of Customers' Wants

Product Selection. Obviously if you don't have what customers want, when they want it, and at an acceptable price, you have not supplied the most basic, but perhaps the most complex to understand, of their wants.

In this chapter I will concentrate on how to improve your assortments to provide more of what your customer wants. Any merchant continually refines his or her product offering. Just deciding to drop one item and buy another is a small step in the process. However, I recommend that you do it in a more formal way, preferably twice a year, before the beginning of the spring and the fall seasons. The methodology will be discussed shortly.

Shopping Convenience. Today's customers are short on time, so the ease of their transactions is paramount. This, of course, embraces a wide variety of things, not the least of which is the ease of checking out. But it also touches everything from location to a myriad of customer-service issues—store layout, displays, and signage, to name just the most obvious.

Peace of Mind. Your customers want to believe that they have purchased the right thing; that it is fairly priced (not necessarily cheap, unless they are price shoppers); that it is not defective; that it is of acceptable quality; and that if something should happen later, you will make good. This requires knowledgeable salespeople who can answer their product questions, can help guide them correctly, and will not oversell the merchandise. As was previously mentioned, it is equally important to have a customer-friendly return policy posted conspicuously in the store.

Some Techniques to Identify Customers' Wants

Before discussing a methodology for refining your product line, let's first consider how you can better understand specifically what your customers want from you. Obviously, analyzing your best sellers will tell you a lot about what your customers like. But there are lots of very fundamental techniques for eliciting evaluations (likes, dislikes, opportunities) from your customers to help you refine both your operation and product line. Not all of the following are applicable to all stores, but from this listing a good many should fit your operation.

Talk to Your Customers. This is a key step in finding out how they feel about your store. This is an important area in which you, the independent retailer, decidedly have the upper hand over the larger chain stores, because you are usually on the floor working with your customers a large part of every day. Buyers for large retailers are so busy today serving the needs of their many stores that they almost never go onto the selling floor to meet their customers.

I can vividly remember being promoted to a buyer position at Bloomingdale's in the 1960s when, in addition to the flagship store at Fifty-Ninth Street in Manhattan, Bloomies had only three branch stores. In those days, Bloomingdale's buyers were required to spend the mornings working on their sales floors and serving their customers. When I was told this was part of my job, I was horrified. "But I am a buyer!" I exclaimed. "I should be buying merchandise, not waiting on customers!" My boss admonished me by telling me it was an important part of my job and I would see.

Well, I did see. And it didn't take long. I got to know my customers, what they liked, and what they didn't. Most important of all, I learned what my customers wanted that I didn't have for them. I listened to them very carefully and moved as quickly as I could to supply what they wanted—within the realm of what I was permitted to buy, of course. The end result was that I was promoted to the next job less than one year later because I had the largest percentage increase of any buyer that year.

So, talk to your customers at every opportunity, and informally interview them about your store, its wares, your customer service, and your competitors. When not selling, take time to walk the floor and introduce yourself to your customers and ask them what they like about your store and what they don't. Encourage your sales staff to do the same and report back to you what they have heard. Keep notes and review suggestions on an ongoing basis.

Buyers from larger operations often rely only on their selling reports, which tell them a lot about what the customer likes, but only evaluate the products that are in stock—nothing else. These reports do not reveal what the store doesn't carry or, just as important, how the customers feel about the shopping experience.

It is also surprising how much information you can gather about your competitors by talking to customers, since most people are only too happy to offer an opinion if asked. Good and natural questions to pose to your customers as you are consummating a sale concern where else they shop for items similar to those they are buying from you, and how they feel in general about your competition.

Customer Complaints. Although no one likes them, addressing customer complaints is an excellent way to refine your business. Only a small portion of customers who are disgruntled actually take the time to complain, but those who do usually have something to say that can often be an impetus for improving something in your operation. Obviously, you should move rapidly to correct any problems that can be resolved. As an aside, a follow-up letter thanking your complaining customers will go a long way toward soothing their feathers, and ensuring that they will come back to your store again.

Post Signs Asking for Customer Feedback. This feedback should concern customer service, merchandise assortment, and so on. The more feedback you can get from your customers, the more you can begin to see your store through their eyes, and the more likely you are to find areas that could use improvement.

Provide Comment Cards. Placing comment cards at the checkout register encourages customers to express their feelings about your store and what could be improved to make their shopping experience more enjoyable. Keep it simple. Ask your customers to rate your store as "Outstanding," "Satisfactory," or "Needs improvement" on the various basic issues of merchandise selection, pricing, merchandise availability, customer service, store ambience, and so on. You will find very good basic cards at the checkout register in virtually every grocery store. Collect a few and adapt them to your needs.

Develop a Questionnaire. If your operation is big enough, develop a questionnaire and leave it near the checkout area, or if possible, have one of your employees administer it to customers at key selling times. Include basic questions about how your customers feel about your store and your product offering. Ask specifically for areas they would like to see improved, such as products and service. It is a good idea to give your participants a small gift, perhaps a coupon offering them a discount on their next purchase.

Conduct a Focus Group. Gather feedback from both customers and noncustomers. Identify several questions to explore for about an hour and gather a group of eight to ten people. Ask them what they like about the store and why they shop there, or why they don't. Ask what else they would like to see you carry or provide, and how they feel about your service. Don't forget to thank them for their participation by giving them a small gift.

Any of these are tools that, properly interpreted, will help you understand better what your customers want—and that is the first step in delivering it!

Review Your Product Assortment

Now that you have talked to your customers, and revisited and refined your strategic mission or message, it is time to review your product line to see if it meshes with your findings, and to decide what changes should be made to make it even more appealing to your target customers.

Categories Appropriate? Do all the categories you carry support your strategic message, or have you picked up some extraneous ones along the way? This is one of the biggest errors retailers often make. It is very easy to do, especially if you have a gift store, because theoretically anything can be a gift. Some categories, however, will coexist more compatibly in your store and enhance the cohesiveness of your total offering more than others. As an example, even though you might be able to sell some, a line of men's tools would look quite out of place in a store that features fine tabletop and porcelain gifts, though a line of fine fragrances or lovely candies would not.

Conversely, are there any categories important to your overall merchandising statement that you are missing and should begin to cultivate? Because it is also important to limit the number of categories you carry, if you want to add a new category, think about whether there are any that you can discontinue. Obviously, the larger the store, the greater the opportunity for additional categories, but too many categories or discordant categories only tend to confuse the overall perception of your store to your customers.

A narrower and more cohesive category statement will make your store appear as complete and easy-to-understand, and will convey to your customers in an instant what your store is all about.

Items on Target? Are the items within each classification targeted to your defined customer?

- Does the style of the item—traditional, contemporary, fashion-forward, or plain vanilla—reflect your customer?
- Is the quality commensurate with what your customer would expect to give, receive, or own?
- Do you have enough items within the category to make a statement?
- Are the products in your store sufficiently different one from the other to give the customer a choice, or is there redundancy, which, if pruned, would result in more openness to buy for other items?

Pricing Fair and Consistent? Is your pricing fair, and does it reflect the perceived value of the item? As was mentioned earlier, specialty stores cannot offer the lowest price in town because of the smaller quantities they buy, the higher freight they pay, and the cost of the extra services that they offer, nor do their customers expect this. But what they do expect and respond to is a consistent pricing policy and a fair pricing policy.

More broadly, ask yourself if there is an overall price consistency in your store (discussed at length in chapter 3), and if there is also a price consistency in the items within each classification. In order to make an assortment within a category, you need either a number of items at difference prices or several items at one price. Most retailers try to work toward price points such as a series of items at $29.95 or a series of items at graduating price points reflecting a "good, better, best" kind of philosophy. It could be a range of items at $9.99, $14.99, and $19.99 as an example, with the $9.99 item being the "good," the $14.99 being the "better," and the $19.99 being the "best."

Compatible and Synergistic? Finally, is each item compatible and synergistic with the rest of your offerings? The more merchandise that is visually compatible, the better the impression your store will make, and the greater the ability for add-on sales you will have.

This, of course, is one reason many retailers develop color stories and themes for each major season so that portions of the store, if not the overall store, have a coordinated and homogeneous look and appear fresh and new. For clothing stores, the changing seasons create changes for the shopkeeper and happen almost in spite of the retailer. For other retailers, especially those in the home business, most seasonal changes require more thought and planning.

As an example, I believe no one in the home business does color stories better than Crate&Barrel, which succeeds on a scale that is not practical for most independent retailers, yet is certainly noteworthy. They develop their own color palettes, different for each season, so their stores constantly look fresh and invite the customer to visit and discover what is new each season. When they make one of their major seasonal changes, the whole store looks just-opened, almost brand-new. While Crate is always either creating its own trends or reflecting emerging trends, I have never seen the company repeat a color scheme in all the many, many years I have been shopping them. Their stores always virtually sing with their fresh, ever-changing palettes.

When it comes to seasonal themes, I think another home furnishings champion is Williams-Sonoma, where the themes are carried throughout the store, from their assortment of gift housewares to specially designed gift packages to coordinated food tastings. They have developed their seasonal stories, many of which have become classics with them, almost to an art form.

Both operations have created fabulous-looking, unique stores. They are retailing theater at its best, providing a reason for their customers to shop them frequently for an abundance of fresh, unique, and new merchandise—designed also to stimulate add-on sales.

No matter what your business, even if it is not in home furnishings, both of these home-specialty retailers are worth a visit at the beginning of a new season just for inspiration and to see how unique and fashionable a store can be with what some might erroneously consider less-fashionable and less-trendy merchandise categories.

Now let's put it all together and talk about how to refine your assortments using the technique known as the style-out. Although one usually thinks of ready-to-wear in connection with style-outs, they can be enormously useful in just about any classification, as we will illustrate with a home category.

How to Conduct a Style-Out

Assemble One of Each Item. After you have selected the category, start by assembling one of each item (or a photo of each) in the category and line them up by price point (lowest to highest usually makes the most sense).

Stand Back and Look at the Collection. The most amazing things become apparent when you look at a typical lineup that you would never notice if the items were scattered about the store, even in close proximity to each other. Ask yourself the following questions:

1. **Is there redundancy?** Items too much like each other only split sales. This is a very common mistake, as most of us tend to buy the same things, or variations thereof, over and over again.
2. **Are there inequities in the pricing?** Something priced out of kilter with the rest of the collection will probably not sell as it should. That is, a comparable item that is priced very much higher than the rest will not usually sell as well as the others, while an underpriced item may outsell all the rest.
3. **What are your overall impressions?** Perhaps "This is one boring assortment" or "My heavens, I had no idea there was so much blue in this lineup." This is where the gold is buried. As many times as I have done style-outs, this is the part that always amazes me. The most astounding things become apparent when one views a classification in this manner.

Arrange the Items by Dollar Sales—this time, highest to lowest, from best sellers to poorest producers. This will enable you to pick out those attributes that make your best sellers, best sellers. The ones at the head of the line will exhibit something in common. It might be price, functionality, design, color, or any combination thereof.

Stand Back and See What Conclusions Become Obvious. The reasons why your best sellers are best sellers should become apparent, which can help you in future product selections. Often, too, they will lead you to other very valid and actionable conclusions, such as line extensions or product voids you could be filling.

Style-outs also yield important clues to understanding your customers' wants. The more style-outs you do, the closer you will come to understanding them, because after a while common themes will begin to emerge. The more of these attributes that you can identify, the easier it will become to pick items your customers will like, want, and buy.

Sally and Sam's Mug Line: An Example Style-Out

Sally and Sam have a small housewares/gift store and have decided to do a style-out of their mug assortment, excluding mugs that are part of dinnerware sets. They have assembled their present freestanding assortment, which consists of sixteen SKUs, ranging from $3.00 to $15.00. The assortment looks okay to them, but they believe they could be doing more mug business in general.

The Assortment by Price. Next they lined up the mugs, starting with the least expensive one as follows:

"S & S" MUG PROGRAM—BY PRICE

	DESCRIPTION	COLOR	PRICE	#	TOTAL	BODY
1	Glass Can Mug	Clear	$3	50	$150	Glass
2	Glass Pedestal Mug	Clear	$4	52	$208	Glass
3	Glass Pedestal Mug	Blue	$4	16	$64	Glass
4	Glass Pedestal Mug	Brown	$4	30	$120	Glass
5	Matt/Shaped	White	$5	40	$200	Ceramic
6	Matt/Shaped	Black	$5	32	$160	Ceramic
7	Stacking	White	$6	50	$300	Porcelain
8	Can	White	$6	10	$60	Ceramic
9	Can	Black	$6	22	$132	Ceramic
10	Can	Red	$6	4	$24	Ceramic
11	Can	Navy	$6	21	$126	Ceramic
12	Can	Yellow	$6	10	$60	Ceramic
13	Flair Handled Can	White	$10	4	$40	Ceramic
14	Hand Painted Fruit	Multi	$10	20	$200	Ceramic
15	Hand Painted Footed	Multi	$12	8	$96	Ceramic
16	Embossed Pedestal	White	$15	4	$60	Ceramic
	TOTAL			373	$2,000	

S&S Mug Program by Lowest Price (Items 1-7)

S&S Mug Program by Lowest Price Continued (Items 8-16)

Review of Lineup by Price. As they reviewed their lineup, they first concluded the pricing was appropriate. The simpler mugs were the least expensive, while the more ornate ones were priced higher.

They also felt they had a good mixture of materials, which included glass, ceramic, earthenware, and porcelain. In addition, they noted a good variety in design—from stacking mugs to can-shape, to mugs with a pedestal foot—with ones that were clear, white, solid colored, or patterned, both painted and in relief. Overall it looked like a pretty good assortment, since it didn't appear to have any obvious voids, redundancies, or inconsistencies.

Line Up by Best Sellers. Next, when they lined up the mugs from best seller to poorest seller, some interesting things became obvious.

"S & S" MUG PROGRAM—BY SALES

	DESCRIPTION	COLOR	PRICE	#	TOTAL	BODY
1	Stacking	White	$6	50	$300	Porcelain
2	Glass Pedestal Mug	Clear	$4	52	$208	Glass
3	Matt/Shaped	White	$5	40	$200	Ceramic
4	Hand Painted Fruit	Multi	$10	20	$200	Ceramic
5	Matt/Shaped	Black	$5	32	$160	Ceramic
6	Glass Can Mug	Clear	$3	50	$150	Glass
7	Can	Black	$6	22	$132	Ceramic
8	Can	Navy	$6	21	$126	Ceramic
9	Glass Pedestal Mug	Brown	$4	30	$120	Glass
10	Hand Painted Footed	Multi	$12	8	$96	Ceramic
11	Glass Pedestal Mug	Blue	$4	16	$64	Glass
12	Can	White	$6	10	$60	Ceramic
13	Can	Yellow	$6	10	$60	Ceramic
14	Embossed Pedestal	White	$15	4	$60	Ceramic
15	Flair Handled Can	White	$10	4	$40	Ceramic
16	Can	Red	$6	4	$24	Ceramic
	TOTAL			373	$2,000	

Immediately they noted that nine of the sixteen SKUs each produced over $120 in sales and that the sixteen together produced $1,596, or just short of 80 percent of the total $2,000 of the classification, so they first concentrated on them to determine the elements that made for their success.

S&S Mug Program by Highest Sales (Items 1-9)

Conclusions: Best Sellers. These are the results Sally and Sam discovered:

1. The white porcelain stacking mug, although not the cheapest, is the best seller. It is extremely basic, at home in most environments. It is made of porcelain, not earthenware, which makes it sleeker and more durable. It also stacks, requiring minimum storage space and making it the perfect extra mug for entertaining.
2. The second-best seller is the clear pedestal mug. This mug is very practical, as the foot negates the need for a coaster. Since it is clear, it also fits into any color scheme. Finally, it is oversized, which is both fashionable and functional.
3. Mugs 3 and 5, the shapely matte-finished mugs, though available only in solid black or white, have appeal because of their graceful and fashionable design and finish.
4. The surprise is the hand-painted fruit motif mug, which is tied for third place with the white matte shapely mug at $200 in sales. Even though it is priced at $10, it is a good value since it is not only very pretty and nicely colored but is hand painted as well.
5. The clear glass basic can (#6), although bland, is probably bought in multiples for entertaining, which accounts for its high sales ranking in the mug assortment.

After the analysis of their best sellers, Sam and Sally concluded that the key elements were mainly functionality, good design, and the ability to fit into most environments—hardly a surprise for a basic mug collection, a large portion of which would be purchased as extras for entertaining.

They also concluded from the surprising sales of their hand-painted mug (#3) that they might have an opportunity in better, more unique, giftable mugs, offered at affordable prices.

Styled-Out Mugs. Next they decided to discontinue the seven poorer-selling mugs, which had not produced even $100 in sales during this period, and to look for a few new ones at the upcoming market to freshen the assortment. So next, in hopes of improving their new selections, they studied the styled-out mugs to determine why they had performed so poorly.

S&S Styled-Out Mugs (Items 10 -16)

As they looked at these discontinued mugs one by one in retrospect, it was easy to see why they did not make the cut. They were too expensive, boring, redundant, or not the right shade/color. The red can was definitely yesterday's red, and the blue of the glass pedestal was not a pleasing shade of blue.

Line Extension. Finally, in addition to replacing some of the styled-out mugs, Sally and Sam decided to use some of the funds and space freed up from the discontinued mugs to test a couple of short, fun, giftable mug collections as a line extension of their mug category.

They ultimately bought two different collections, which they phased in throughout the year. The first collection featured screen-printed cartoons and unique packaging that made them even more desirable gifts, while the second collection depicted characters designed for kids. Each collection was extremely successful.

To keep the mug momentum going, Sally and Sam are doing another mug style-out (one year after the first) to free up some more funds. In addition, based on the success of their mug program (including the gift mug sets), for their next buying trip they are transferring more funds to this category from another poorer-performing classification.

Review Your Best Sellers and Markdowns

While it might seem obvious that your best sellers and your poorer sellers (markdowns) can help you a great deal in refining your product line, few merchants I have known really maximize these simple tools.

As you review your selling reports or conduct style-outs, think about your best sellers and see what commonalities you can find among them. These items may be particularly well priced, the most fashionable, the most basic, the newest, from a particular vendor, or perhaps a combination of these things—but over time you will see that they will fall more into one category than another. If you analyze your best sellers periodically in this light, you should find some very interesting clues to picking best sellers in the future.

While few of us want to concentrate on our markdowns, because they usually are evidence of poor buys we made, they can also yield some surprising conclusions, which can improve future buys, if we face them squarely and categorize them in a similar manner to the best sellers.

In summary, refining your store and your product line calls for constant vigilance, analysis, and learning; but this, in my opinion, is one of the more interesting things about retailing. There is always something to learn, and something to improve, to make your store more profitable.

CHAPTER 10

Maximizing a Trade Show or Buying Trip

You can do a number of things to make a buying trip more productive and efficient, starting with planning it. As they say, "Nothing succeeds like a good plan."

Preparing for a Buying Trip

In addition to attending to the travel details, to maximize a buying trip and to keep yourself focused, it is essential to develop a shopping list and a rough buy plan before you leave.

Traveling Details and Making Reservations. If you are traveling out of town, make all your reservations early: plane, hotel, rental car, and so on. By planning ahead you can often take advantage of specials that may not be available later; and you may even be able to book a hotel room close to where you will be shopping, which you will find a great advantage when you arrive. When placing reservations in advance, however, be sure you understand fully what is involved if you have to cancel. With trade shows some hotels may not refund the room charges if a reservation is canceled shortly before the event starts.

Register in advance for the show. Also, if you are attending a trade show, register early for it and for any seminars or meetings that you would like to attend. You will save valuable time later on and be assured of a place in some events that might be closed by the time you arrive at the show.

Documents that you may need should be checked and assembled well in advance. If you are traveling abroad, for example, check to see that your passport is up-to-date and be sure you have any visas, as well as any shots, required to enter any of the countries in which you will be traveling.

For any buying trip, assemble all documents and information that you might need for placing orders, such as plenty of business cards, credit references, your resale certificate, and tax number.

Review catalogs and websites, and make appointments before you arrive. If you are attending a trade show, check the catalog and pertinent websites in advance to help determine what or whom you may want to see. After you have assembled your shopping list, which I will discuss shortly, make appointments with your more important vendors in advance.

Packing appropriately is another key consideration. When packing for the show or trip, bear in mind that your appearance will affect how some vendors treat you and also how you feel about yourself. Start with taking the most comfortable shoes you own. Nothing can make a buying trip more miserable than feet that hurt, as many of us gals can tell you having learned to save the high heels for later.

Second, I strongly recommend you dress in business casual attire. I can tell you firsthand that when I was a senior vice president for a major furniture manufacturer, at the big shows in High Point, North Carolina, when dealers entered the showroom in outlandish costumes, often Western outfits when they were not from Texas, I immediately thought they were small dealers trying to make an impression. They made an impression all right, but I don't think the result was what they wanted. As often as not, I would shuffle them off to one of my junior salespeople to save our real pros for a serious-looking buyer who might enter the showroom any minute.

With all the extra charges the airlines have today, it is wise to travel as light as possible; also be sure to leave some extra room in your suitcases. On most buying trips you will amass pamphlets, catalogs, fliers, and even possibly some small samples. While some suppliers will mail these items home for you, most will not, so it is wise to come prepared.

Reviewing Your Assortments and Preparing a Shopping List. This is a very important step in maximizing a buying trip. First, you should review any trend information you may have developed. With that in mind, review your categories and your best sellers within each category to determine where you may have voids that you might fill at this market.

Set goals for your trip, being as specific as you can. Detail the targeted items you need to augment your present assortment, including how much they should cost or sell for. Tally up the approximate cost of purchasing an appropriate stock of each, if you find them.

Review your slow sellers to help you determine if there are any you should try to replace. If there are, be as specific as you can about a replacement and try to put a dollar amount on purchasing each proposed new item. Adding up the two lists will give you a first draft open-to-buy (or purchasing budget) for the buying trip.

Prioritize your list of items, and ask yourself if you could afford to buy all of these items if you found them. If the answer is no, review your list and prioritize the items from most important to least important, removing any that no longer look so important. Then make another list of what you would discontinue and sell through if you were lucky enough to find everything on your new shopping list.

Reconcile your lists by eliminating the lowest items on either list until the list of what you can afford is consistent with the funds you can free up. This will give you a shopping list and a rough open-to-buy. Remember, though, the new orders will have to be staged commensurate with the timing of the availability of funds, often to be collected from selling your discontinued items.

Setting a Schedule and Making Appointments. As was mentioned previously, it is a good idea to make appointments with your key vendors in advance of your trip. You will avoid having to stop by more than once because they are working with another retailer when you show up; and you will also appear more professional. To do this properly you should do the following:

List your key suppliers/locations, and on your list note briefly if you have anything special to discuss with each that might require additional time for the appointment. After checking their locations re-sort your list by location. If you are attending a trade show, you don't want to be running from aisle to aisle and then retracing your steps for the next appointment if you can avoid it. Or if you are attending a market in a city like New York, which might be in several buildings, be sure you know which buildings your suppliers are in before you end up burning time and money on extra cab rides or wearing yourself out backtracking and running from building to building.

Note your contact. This is important. Not only is it embarrassing if you get to a vendor with whom you have done business before and cannot remember the name of your rep, but it also makes you look like an amateur.

Add new vendors. If you are attending a trade show or market that has been covered by the trade magazines, be sure to read them to identify any new vendors you may want to add to your shopping list and plug those in. Also add to this list any other vendors you have heard about or those who have sent a rep to visit you (as long as you feel those vendors may have possibilities). For many buyers this is not a priority, but in my mind finding new suppliers is one of the most important goals for most buying trips, especially for trade shows.

There are two schools of thought about how to use this list and actually shop the market. Some buyers prefer to make appointments only with their important vendors and then walk the market, dropping in on possible new vendors after they have completed their key vendor appointments. Others like to shop a market by location, making appointments with their key vendors and leaving time in between to visit with their new prospects. Either one works to keep you on track and avoids your spending extra time backtracking. Remember also, as was previously recommended, to leave some time to shop the market looking for new trends.

Finally, a shopping trip or attending a trade show can be an exhausting proposition. Therefore, I recommend heartily that you leave small bits of time in your schedule to rest and take breaks. You'll thank yourself at the end of the day.

Keeping a Notebook. It is a good idea to start a new "notebook" (either on paper or via the electronic device of your choosing) for each market, trade show, or major market trip. You might be surprised to find out how many buyers think this is unnecessary, but from my years of experience I can vouch for the fact that keeping complete notes is essential to maximizing any buying trip, and those notes will usually be referenced many times later.

However you are keeping your notes, first insert your shopping list and your market schedule, complete with each vendor's name and phone number (it is only courteous and professional to try to be on time, but if you are really running late, you should call ahead to let the vendor know).

It is a good idea to create a template to facilitate keeping your notes on important items. I found how important this could be when I was a furniture buyer for Bloomingdale's, because there were so many things I needed to know about a new item before I could calculate its total cost to set the retail. For example, as was previously mentioned, in the furniture business, the freight factor is such a large percentage of the cost that you have to calculate it pretty accurately or you can be way off on your markup. You need to know the FOB point (point at which you assume ownership and responsibility for the freight), the item's weight, the size of the carton, the freight rate from the FOB point, whether you will fill a whole truck or whether it will go the more expensive LTL way (less than a truckload). I made a cheat sheet (a preprinted page) for the necessary details on the items I was really interested in buying. This ensured that I never left a vendor and had to call or e-mail later for some vital piece of information I was missing—which is particularly important when making a foreign buying trip.

To the degree that you want to leave with everything you need to know to place an order, or want to remember all the important questions to ask about each item, you can create a version of the page below with the things that are important to you.

New Item Page Example:

WINTER MARKET	_____, 20 __
Vendor	
Description:	
Colors:	
Sizes:	
Pre-packs:	
FOB:	
Freight Allowance:	
Advertising Allowance:	
Other:	

Shopping the Market

Like for everything else, there is a better way and a not-so-good way to shop a market. In addition to making your shopping list and setting an efficient schedule, your goal should be to have equally efficient vendor meetings so you can accomplish as much as possible in the time available. I cannot remember having visited a trade show or made a major buying trip for which I could not have used more time, so being efficient can really be important.

The Vendor Meeting. I have often visited a market with young buyers who really don't know what to ask, or what to ask for, much beyond the price of the item in which they have some interest. Left to their own devices, they would not have gotten nearly as much out of each vendor meeting as they should have. Depending upon one's business, the list of questions varies enormously, but there are a few key areas that should usually be probed.

Qualifying a new vendor is an important step if it is a new vendor, or one with whom you are barely familiar. After a cursory review of his or her line to ensure that there are items that might be of interest, spend a few minutes right up front getting to know something about his or her credentials to determine if this vendor is right for you.

Perhaps most important to determine is who the vendor's biggest customers are. This will classify him or her pretty accurately and very quickly as to whether he or she should be in your stable of suppliers. Obviously if you have a small boutique and the vendor tells you Walmart is his or her biggest customer, thank the vendor and go on your way because the chances are overwhelmingly against you that the supplier's wares will suit your needs as a small independent shopkeeper. Or, if you are a middle-of-the-road shop and his or her largest customers are very chic shops, this vendor may not be worth trying to develop. Along these same lines, find out which of your competitors the vendor serves in your area and which are most important to him or her. This will give you some idea of how important you could become to this supplier.

Cutting to the chase, the next most important task is to find out what sorts of minimums are required, if any, per order. This will tell you immediately if you can do business with the supplier. If his or her minimums are just too high, you'll know it can't work with this vendor at this stage of your business and that it is time to move on.

What to ask each vendor is your next area of concern. After you have qualified the new vendor as someone with whom you would like to do business, or if you are meeting with an existing vendor, it is time to select the items of interest and find out if they might be for you. In addition to asking about the pricing, if you are still interested in the item, there is more you may want to determine:

- Has the vendor sold it to anyone else in your marketplace?
- Is the merchandise in stock?
- Can it be reordered?
- What is the reorder time?
- Where does it come from? What is the percent freight to get to you?
- Are there any selling aids for the product?
- What is the average life span of such an item in this line?
- If it doesn't sell, can you exchange it for other merchandise?

And additional things you may want to know about any order you may place include the following:

- What are the vendor's payment terms?
- Is there a trade discount for ordering at market?
- Does the vendor have a co-op advertising program or ad allowance?
- Can you get dating?
- Are there any training materials on this item/line?
- Does the vendor offer any promotions on the line?
- What is the return policy?

Perhaps the last question you might like to ask is how to get a better price. If you have an inclination to bargain, as many buyers do, this will give you an idea if there is any room for this discussion. If not, at least your vendor will know you are on your toes, and you will feel more secure that you have gotten the best price.

Taking Pictures. Over the years I've noted, as was previously mentioned, that one of the most frequent errors that buyers make is to buy versions of the same thing over and over again, especially if they are on a long trip. Also, after a day or so at the market, it is often difficult to remember exactly what that first item you saw yesterday—and were so steamed up about—really looked like. And was it really the right color?

If the item is to fit into one of your themes, presumably you have already checked its compatibility with your Pantone colors, but without a picture most items will fade in your memory in time. It is so important to take a camera (or anything else that will take a picture) to record the items you are interested in.

Digital cameras and the many new handheld electronic devices have made it very easy now. They are small and hassle-free. When you get home, you can print the pictures you want and toss the others, but you can refer back to them as you continue through the market. This is a far cry from the huge Polaroid land cameras and boxes of bulky film we used to carry! On a long trip I usually had a small suitcase just to carry the camera and film that I would need to adequately record my finds. Then I had to wait ten seconds for each picture to develop, not to mention letting them cure for a minute so I could put them away without them all sticking together. After all that, it wasn't even a very good picture—and only black and white at that.

A word of caution, though, about photos. Many trade shows and suppliers forbid you to take pictures. Before taking one, do ask permission. If you are working with a vendor and he or she knows you are serious about an item, you usually will be allowed to take a picture. However, since vendors' biggest fear is that you may show the picture to a competitor who might knock them off, you must assure them that you won't. Then be true to your word, or you will find soon that you are unable to take any more pictures at your biggest vendors.

Writing Orders. Not everyone agrees with me on my position here. Many buyers like to place their orders at market, often before leaving the vendor appointment, so they are finished and can go on to other things. While there are some instances when it is advantageous to place orders at market (perhaps for psychological reasons related to your vendor or for an extra discount for placing an order at market), in the main I disagree.

I have learned that if you can, it is best to take your notes and your pictures at market and defer writing your orders until you have returned home and the dust has settled. Or even better, wait until you have completed the bulk of the markets or vendors for a season. It is time then to review all of your planned purchases in context with each other and within the assortments that you already have. Weed out the items that are either somewhat duplicative or those that no longer look as good to you as they did while you were at market or visiting with your vendors. It is amazing how ugly an item can have become just a short time after you fell in love with it at market! If you can wait for this final review, it is almost guaranteed that your resultant product line will be more cohesive and more tightly knit.

For the items that are to be part of your themes, make sure once more that they really fit, and then add their pictures to your theme boards. This will give you a real preview of how you and your customers will see those stories/trends when you set them up in the store.

One final note on placing your orders: it is best to use your own order forms rather than the vendor's. You will look more professional, and you will avoid the fine print on the vendor's version, which can sometimes be quite confusing or costly.

CHAPTER 11

Getting the Word Out

One of the most critical elements to the success of any retail business is the effectiveness of the marketing program to promote it. It doesn't matter if you have the most wonderful widget in the world if your customers don't know about it.

You have outlined the basics of your marketing plan in your business plan, and perhaps now it is time to flesh it out or reexamine the one you have with new eyes. In this chapter I will aim to hit the basics for traditional advertising media only. The next chapter will be devoted to using the Internet, which has become so powerful in reaching your customers.

Your Marketing Program

I've often thought of the retail marketing plan as a three-legged stool, with the most successful promotional campaigns consisting of three well-developed legs working together: advertising, sales promotion, and public relations. Many people do not know the difference between them, but they are very different, and each can play a vital role in building your business.

- **Advertising.** Generally speaking, this is a paid function (like a TV or radio ad) controlled by the advertiser and used to deliver a *message* widely to build a brand or drive customers to a store or service.
- **Sales Promotion.** This consists of methods or techniques, such as sales, coupons, gifts, rebates, or discounts, that convey *value* to stimulate interest and sales; promotions are normally used in conjunction with the other marketing functions.
- **Public Relations.** PR programs create goodwill or promote a company's products or *image,*_usually through the media, which is free but uncontrolled.

Let's review them, one by one.

Advertising: Creating the Advertising Plan

Since your advertising program will be one of your largest expenses and such a critical element in your success, it is important that you have a sound plan. Unless it is properly planned and executed, there are few places where you can spend so much money and have so little or nothing to show for it. There are several vital steps in creating a successful advertising plan.

Identify and Understand Your Customers. The first step is to identify your customers as accurately and as completely as you can, which is crucial before you decide how and where you will advertise. You need to understand both their demographics (statistical characteristics like age and income) and their psychographics (attitudes and tastes) in order to determine the most efficient means to communicate with them. Will they respond best to newspaper ads? A website? Coupons? You must know the best methods and the best times to approach them if you are to reach your target audience efficiently.

What Do You Want to Say or Accomplish? Obviously you want to communicate your USP (unique selling proposition—what makes you different from your competition), your area of expertise, what you have to offer your customer, and why the customer should come to you. But different ads have disparate goals intending to accomplish diverse things like increasing sales or customer awareness, or perhaps attracting a competitor's customers. It is important that you understand your goals clearly, as well as the messages you want to communicate, as you put your program together. This becomes the foundation for your creative approach.

Establish a Budget. While there are sophisticated methods for establishing an advertising budget, cutting to the chase, most believe that for an independent it should be between 2 percent and 5 percent of your gross sales, with 2 percent being the absolute minimum. It is important that the budget and the program that you establish are sustainable and consistent over a period of time. This is vitally important for the success of any campaign because advertising awareness builds incrementally over time; a shot here and a shot there will have little impact on your audience.

The timing of your advertising expenditures, which will also influence the cost of your ads, is an important part of your budget and plan. You should allocate the bulk of your ads slightly before important business times or specific promotions and when you can reach your targeted customers to get the biggest bang for your buck.

Get Help. Really effective advertising is an art, and some people are very good at it. If you have a sufficient budget, hiring a small advertising agency is usually the best way to get an effective message and the most appropriate media. However, since few independents can afford an agency, working with a freelance copywriter is a good way to hone your message. There are also media buying companies that can help guide you in making efficient media buys.

Furthermore, if you have some talent, there are lots of possibilities for you with all the desktop publishing programs available today, as well as the many Internet sources and adult education courses available to help the novice. Even if you have a way with words, you might consider getting some help, because there are tricks of the trade that could benefit you.

Select Your Best Advertising Alternatives. Whichever advertising medium or combination you select, a major key to success in promoting your business is, as I have mentioned, consistency and frequency of message, so it is imperative that you design a campaign that can be ongoing. Furthermore, your logo and tagline (if you have one) should appear in every communication you have with your customers. The more often they see it, the more likely they are to get to know you and react to your message.

There are many ways to advertise. Some are too expensive to be a major part of a smaller independent retailer's promotional strategy, while others are quite affordable and can be very effective. Each media option has its strengths and weaknesses and may be important, depending on the developmental stage of your business. Normally, though, for an advertising campaign to be effective, you need to employ more than one.

Newspapers are perhaps still the first medium one thinks of in connection with retail advertising today, even with the Internet revolution. Depending on the paper, the city, and the size of the ad, this can be a very effective medium, but also among the most expensive.

The major papers in any locale usually have a pretty wide readership, even if it is on the decline, so a well-targeted ad can produce some very good results. While the ads are usually short-lived because the paper is usually read once and then discarded, because of their frequency, newspapers are ideal for delivering immediate action for events like sales with a specified short life.

Since the major papers are usually too pricey for the independent to sustain in an ongoing campaign, good alternatives are the much cheaper neighborhood or throwaway papers available in most communities.

Magazines can be a very productive method of advertising, provided their readers have the same demographics and interests as your target customer. These ads have a much longer life span and, with their ability to present your message in vivid color, can create impactful impressions. However, the larger national magazines have long lead times, and their ads are very expensive. Again, as in the case of newspapers, many areas have local, usually free, magazines, which might be targeted better for your store and certainly will be more affordable.

Television commercials reach the largest audience and with sight, sound, and movement can be very impactful. They are usually too expensive, between production and time, for any but the biggest events or largest operations and generally reach an audience a good deal wider than one's target.

Radio can be used very effectively to reach a large audience, and because it is so much more affordable than TV, it is often a staple in the media plans of independent shopkeepers. Radio commercials have immediacy and can usually be targeted pretty easily to your desired audience. You must, however, ensure that your ads will air when your customer is listening.

Outdoor advertising or using outdoor billboards can be a very cost-effective way to advertise. Your message must be limited if it is to be intelligible to those driving by. Space on billboards can be bought strategically, though; for example, an ad near your store could offer added impact by inviting your customers to visit. For the more flamboyant at heart, skywriting is another form of outdoor advertising.

The Yellow Pages can be considered as part of your arsenal, depending on your business and how likely your customer is to search there for your kind of store or service.

Posters and bulletin boards can be an effective means of communicating details about special events to your customers if there are bulletin boards around your place of business that allow posters or fliers.

Direct-mail opportunities abound for the independent retailer. While larger retailers periodically send their catalogs and postcards to those on their mailing lists, you can communicate with your customers via direct mail on a regular basis as well. Of course, you must start with a mailing list. It is best to develop your own by signing up customers who come to your store or by taking addresses off their checks. But since it often takes quite a while to build a meaningful list, most independents augment theirs by renting or purchasing names of people whose demographics mirror their customers. Unfortunately these lists tend to get outdated quite quickly, and since the cost of postage is an issue, you need to purge your lists periodically.

Postcards are for many independents (and other retailers as well) the most effective direct-mail opportunity. They are the cheapest to mail, can be very eye-catching, do not need to be opened to relay the message, and can be used to communicate many different types of messages to your customers. If you include a coupon, it will make it easy to track their effectiveness.

By way of illustration, one of the most effective postcard campaigns in many years is the oversized royal-blue postcard that Bed Bath & Beyond sends periodically, offering their customers 20 percent off a single item. It is such an institution now that Bed Bath & Beyond shoppers don't read it anymore; they just put it into their bag for their next visit to the store, which is, as hoped, often spurred by the receipt of the postcard.

Measure the Effectiveness. Finally, you should give some thought to how to measure the success of your advertising expenditures. While there are many sophisticated ways to do this, the most basic method is tracking and comparing your sales, store traffic, or phone calls during your ad period against a similar time the year before; or tracking the sales of an item against its previous unadvertised weekly or monthly sales. You can also ask your customers when they enter your store if they have seen your ad; or you can ask them to bring the ad or a coupon into the store for a reward. If you are working with an agency, they will usually measure the effectiveness of their ads for you using their own techniques.

Tips to Make Your Advertising More Effective

No matter which medium you decide to use, there are certain principles and tricks that should make your advertising (and other forms of promotion) more effective. As was mentioned in the beginning of this chapter, writing really captivating advertising is a real talent, which is why so many firms hire advertising agencies, or at least copywriters, to help them with their advertising messages. The following suggestions, however, are applicable whether you write you own ad, or a friend or copywriter does.

1. **Focus your communication on your target audience.** Develop or hone your own database, or buy or rent lists of customers with demographics that are similar to those of your best customers. For all broadcast media, in addition to selecting the correct target audience, timing the ad to air when it will reach them is crucial. Think about your audience as you create your advertisement, making sure the ad speaks to them and tells them something *they want to hear*, not just something you want to say.

2. **Your headline must grab their attention.** Without a strong beginning, few will read further or pay attention. Many experts think asking a provocative question, making a startling announcement, or introducing your product's benefit with a how-to tip is a good formula for making an enticing headline. Others suggest using "you" in the headline. I suggest that after you know what you want to communicate in the ad, you write as many headlines as you can think of. Write a ton and then review them. Chances are you'll end up with a pretty good headline and one that is probably much better than your first.

3. **Include a picture if you can.** They say a picture is worth a thousand words. Most people in advertising

agree with this. More people will notice a photo or a strong graphic than will read a headline.

4. **Is your message worth communicating?** This is of prime importance. You must make sure that your company or store communicates your unique selling proposition, which sets your operation apart from your competitors. If you are trying to sell a specific product, does the product have a strong and unique enough story of features, advantages, and benefits to make it worthwhile to advertise? If you are announcing a sale, is the message really compelling? If you can't answer yes to these questions, don't bother—you'll probably be throwing your money away.

5. **Your communication must be clear, simple, and understandable.** Often the novice, trying to include everything, is too verbose, which results in an ad with little impact. Keep your sentences short and powerful. Furthermore, especially in radio you must use an economy of words, adding sounds or jingles to grab attention and make up for the lack of visual elements. Leave out trite phrases. Rewrite as often as necessary to get a clear, clean message.

6. **Your message should play on your target audience's emotions.** Touch them where they feel—their wants and their needs—rather than through pure, hard logic. What will your product do for them? Why must they have it?

7. **Be truthful and don't oversell.** Consumers are pretty smart. Nothing will turn them off and make them turn the page faster than making some outrageous claim that they know can't possibly be true. And, of course, there are truth-in-advertising laws. Conversely, if you can include a compelling guarantee, it will add tremendously to your credibility. According to surveys, most people believe an ad that contains a money-back guarantee.

8. **Develop your own advertising personality and copy style—the more likable the better**. Your goal should be that with enough frequency consumers will know it is your ad before they read the copy.

9. **Include a call to action and a sense of urgency.** Tell your target audience what they must do and why they must do it, and include a short timetable in which they must take action. In other words, ask for the order clearly and try to build a fire under them. A discount coupon that is good for only a short period is a proven way to cement the deal.

10. **Make sure your advertising has enough frequency.** Repetition in advertising is a key to success. Usually the more often consumers see your ad, the more of an impression it will make on them.

11. **Your store's name and logo should be prominently displayed with complete contact information.** It sounds obvious that any ad should identify its advertiser, location, and complete contact information. However, I can tell you from years of reading ads that some of the biggest get so swept up in relaying their message that they overlook these details and make the customer search for this vital information (or whatever there is of it).

12. **Ensure that your ad is grammatically correct, free of typos, and professional in every way.** Proofread, proofread, proofread—and then have someone else proofread it. Nothing can cause you to lose credibility faster than to have some real bloopers in your ad.

13. **Test your ads.** If you have developed what you think is a gangbusters ad, try it in a small paper or with a smaller mailing before going whole-hog. If possible, test a couple of permutations at the same time to see which pulls customers in the best.

14. **Try different media and different types of ads.** There's a whole world of advertising possibilities out

there. Try different formats. In time you will learn what is the most effective for you, and you may find some happy surprises along the way.

15. **Track the results and study why some of your ads are more successful than others.** Since successful advertising is normally a function of repetition, the more you can learn from your successes and failures, the more effective your future advertising should be.

16. **Don't tire prematurely of good ads**. Another mistake that is often made is thinking that each ad should be new and fresh. While you certainly can run an ad into the ground, good ads can be repeated many times before they become stale and, as was already mentioned, usually will provide better and better results as they are rerun. This, of course, is another reason to track your results to measure their effectiveness—acceptable, building, or waning.

Sales Promotion Opportunities

In addition to direct advertising, there are many opportunities to promote your store, your products, and your services, using various sales promotion techniques. While advertising is primarily an external, paid form of communication to the masses, sales promotion techniques are more limited in exposure and are normally used internally to heighten interest and promote sales of a product or service. There are many promotional tactics that can be employed effectively and reasonably to increase awareness and sales.

The Basics. Some are so simple as to be often overlooked.

Business cards are a great example not always appreciated for their effectiveness. Designed for your store with your logo and tagline (if you have one), they are great silent salespeople that should be readily available in your store. Give them out whenever you can to whomever you can; and also inquire around town if you may leave some in other businesses that cater to a similar clientele.

Gift boxes, gift certificates, and shopping bags with your logo and store graphics can strongly promote your store. Your gift boxes and gift certificates may well be an introduction to a new customer, so they should be designed with care as part of your overall graphics presentation.

As a testament to just how effective one of these sales promotion techniques can be, few might remember what I believe started the first shopping-bag craze fifty years ago. In 1961 Bloomingdale's launched its second big storewide event, "Espirit de France." To help promote the event, the company designed a shopping bag that sported huge tarot cards in red, white, and black—but included no store name! This shopping bag became the rage. All the trendsetting New Yorkers just had to have one and within a couple of months the bag could be seen being carried by consumers all over the world, and everyone knew the unidentified tarot card shopping bag came from Bloomingdale's. Now most stores have their own shopping bags, and Bloomingdale's has their Big Brown Bag, which is probably nearly as famous as their tarot card bags.

Every piece of "paper" that you generate, whether physical or electronic—stationery, bills you send out, e-mails, store questionnaires—should have your company name, logo, and tagline prominently displayed on them. They are all salespeople for your business.

Brochures and fliers can be created about your offerings. Today, with the PC and all the advanced desktop publishing programs, it is relatively easy and cost-effective to produce all kinds of promotional takeaways. Educational brochures can explain and create more interest in the items you sell, and fliers can herald any number of events you may have in your store. While these can be very effective for in-store placement or can be used as bag stuffers to promote your store and your products, they can also be mailed or e-mailed directly to your customers.

A newsletter that you or your staff writes makes a terrific promotional tool to mail or e-mail to your customers, or to provide in your store. When I was the president of Workbench, a contemporary furniture specialty store, we had a monthly newsletter (written and produced by the owner's wife), which told the customer interesting facts about furniture and furnishing a home. Our customers loved it and looked forward to receiving it every month—as we learned from the numerous complaints we received on the rare occasions when it was late or we skipped a month.

In-Store Promotional Events. These give you an opportunity to communicate with your customers, inviting them into your store to hopefully increase sales. Most of these events, as great promotional opportunities, will become central elements in your advertising and your public relations campaigns.

Again, a bit of retail history: In 1960 (the year I joined Bloomingdale's to begin my retail career) the company produced its first promotion, called "Casa Bella," which celebrated Italian craftsmanship and featured exclusive merchandise from all over Italy. A special series of shops took over a large piece of real estate from the furniture floor on the fifth floor, and small outposts were created in many departments throughout the store. As the years went by, the promotions got bigger, and bigger, and bigger, and the term *retailing as theater* began to be used to describe Bloomingdale's annual promotions. The retail community saw the potency of these galas, and although it is now done mostly on a much more modest scale, retailers today have promotions for every possible occasion to lure customers into their stores.

You need not, like Bloomingdale's, shop the globe for new themes. In order to maximize this opportunity, you can develop a monthly calendar to ensure that you have something happening often. Starting with the annual calendar of holiday and national events, you will have a framework of at least one no-brainer theme to build your events and promotions around each month. The most obvious themes by month are:

- **January:** New Year's Day, Super Bowl, and Martin Luther King Day
- **February:** Groundhog Day, Mardi Gras, Presidents' Day, and Valentine's Day
- **March:** St. Patrick's Day, First Day of Spring, Passover, and Easter (both sometimes in April)
- **April:** April Fool's Day, Tax Day, and Earth Day
- **May:** Mother's Day, National Teacher Day, and Memorial Day
- **June:** Father's Day, Flag Day, and Graduation
- **July:** Independence Day
- **August:** Back to School
- **September:** Labor Day and Grandparents Day
- **October:** Columbus Day, World Series, National Boss Day, and Halloween
- **November:** Election Day, Veterans Day, Thanksgiving, and Black Friday
- **December:** Christmas and New Year's Eve

On top of this basic framework, create your own promotional events and layer them on to your monthly calendar where most appropriate or when needed to stimulate some extra business.

Special sales like a One-Day Sale, Customer Appreciation Day, or Anniversary Sale during which you offer some extraordinary values can stimulate a lot of extra business.

Product demonstrations can often be done by vendors' reps. Cooking demos to showcase various cooking utensils are a prime example of frequently held, very popular demonstrations.

A celebrity visit to your store can often increase traffic. Depending on your business category, different types of famous personalities may have appeal. Perhaps the best example of this strategy is an author who comes to your local bookstore to autograph his or her book. Your vendors are often able to supply someone of interest, or there may be a local resident whom your customers might like to meet—perhaps an actor or actress.

Have a special shopping night when your store is not normally open, to accommodate your customers who cannot usually come during your regular shopping hours. Make the event more special by serving refreshments and adding whatever else you can to give the night a celebratory feeling, like live music or a celebrity guest.

A local charity day, for which you partner with a local charity and donate a percentage of your sales during the event, is perhaps one of the most effective promotions a local retailer can have. Everyone would like to do some good and be charitable and this offers them the opportunity to kill two birds with one stone. They buy something they would like and, at the same time, make a contribution to charity. This is a "win-win" situation for all involved.

A national charity event is a variation on this theme. An example would be a tie-in with the Red Cross in which you contribute an amount from each sale to aid people after a flood, hurricane, or some other natural disaster, as many retailers did after the massive 2011 earthquake in Japan.

Contests or drawings in which you offer prizes to the winning customers provide an extra benefit. Usually the customer has to fill in an entry blank, which is an excellent way of adding him or her to your mailing list.

Bonuses to your customers when they buy a certain amount of a particular product or products can help you increase your average sale. The old "Buy two and get one free" promotion really does work.

Coupons usually offer your customers a discounted price on specific items or a certain percent off on particular items or on their total sale. This is one of the most widely used techniques, as you can't help but notice when you stand behind someone in the checkout line at the grocery store who is redeeming a particularly big fistful of coupons.

Gifts with purchase reward your customers with a little something extra when they purchase a specified item. The gift is often made available by the manufacturer. Perhaps the best example of gift-with-purchase rewards is found in the cosmetics industry, when several times a year the better lines offer specially designed, very attractive cosmetic bags filled with sampler-size cosmetics and perfumes. We gals usually wait with great anticipation to receive these from our favorite brands.

Giveaways like pens, mouse pads, calendars, and coffee mugs with your store's name and logo on them are always popular. Just about everyone likes a freebie and will usually take one even if they don't really want it. This is a very good way of thanking your customers for their patronage, setting you apart from your competition, and getting your name and logo out there.

All of these promotional events should help you boost traffic, and with increased traffic should come additional sales.

Public Relations

Free Publicity. Often, too, events are noteworthy enough for you to get free publicity from your local media, which can often be even more effective and credible than your own advertising because someone else is saying it. This is public relations in a nutshell.

Public relations can be a very important tool for the independent retailer to ultimately increase sales. While it surely is a very cost-effective way to introduce you to new customers and reinvigorate old customers, the only real downside is that unlike for traditional advertising, you cannot control the message or edit what is said. The press, at their discretion, will take whatever stand they wish to make it a more exciting story. While you can never be sure what this will be, most people are more than willing to take the risk for the free "advertising" that can be so effective, but you do have to be prepared for the unexpected.

To this day I remember vividly a very embarrassing experience I had many years ago when I was the modern-furniture buyer at Bloomingdale's. I was married to an entrepreneur who was very involved in real estate. We had two homes: one in Manhattan and the other a beach house next to the ocean on Fire Island.

My husband was very good at getting publicity, and at first I enjoyed the limelight too. Then a very famous writer for the *New York Times* interviewed us in both our houses and wrote an almost full-page article on our lifestyle as a young modern New York couple. As I went to work that Saturday morning, I picked up the paper to read our article, which was complete with four big pictures of both houses, including our pet dog and cat, Moose and Clyde. I nearly had a heart attack. The article was headlined, "Next Time She'll Do Away with Furniture." It went on to read, "Next time around Jody Bradshaw, Bloomingdale's modern-furniture buyer intends to build a house that requires no furniture." Stanley, my husband, had said that, not me. You can imagine my concern for how Bloomingdale's management might react to this.

When I got to my office, the phone was ringing. Much to my horror, Marvin Traub, the president of Bloomingdale's, was on the line. "Congratulations," he said. "That was some article. I just love articles that will get people talking." I was very relieved he took that stance and very grateful not to have been fired, but after that I realized that PR can be a double-edged sword. Consider the other side of the coin, though—imagine what a 7/8-page ad in the *New York Times* on a Saturday would cost, even then!

Techniques for Getting Free PR. Your public relations calendar should be planned to be an integral part of your promotional calendar. Begin by identifying your objectives—what you want to accomplish, how you want your operation to be perceived, and what messages you want to convey. With this in hand you can begin to find the opportunities to plan and the tools to implement a successful PR campaign in your community.

While most larger organizations have their own public relations person or department, many shopkeepers in the early stages of their businesses find it to be a worthwhile investment to hire a freelance PR person who knows the ropes and knows the members of the local press, and who can pave the way and discover what works best for their businesses.

There are many ways to get you and your business noticed and promoted in your community, some of which I just noted in the discussion of sales promotion events, but there are so many more to be considered.

Develop a press kit and distribute it to the media at every opportunity for which you have some reason to contact them— and keep it updated and fresh.

Send press releases to your local paper when you have anything meaningful to announce, like special events of interest, noteworthy new products, or a meaningful new service.

Write a newsletter, as was previously suggested, for your customers and distribute it widely. You can, of course, include news about your company; but trends in the market, new innovations, or anything of a broader scope that might interest your reader will make it more desirable.

Hold a monthly clinic or how-to seminar related to your products that will give your customers a reason to visit your shop and also, perhaps even more important, help you or your operation become known as an expert in your area.

Write articles for the local paper on your area of expertise. Local newspapers and magazines are generally hungry for this type of material.

Tie-in with a charity in any number of ways. Donate products to a local charitable event, or donate part of every sale to a national well-known charity.

Join a trade association or the chamber of commerce, and be a real participating member to become known as a mover and shaker and a well-respected tradesperson in your community.

Volunteer for various community services.

Participate in seminars, and look for opportunities to be on a local *radio talk show.*

Build relationships with other businesses in town that cater to the same clientele, and partner with them to put on events.

Identify your business on your vehicles, especially any van you may use for deliveries, but even your personal car can exhibit special license plates that identify you.

As you begin to think about your business, other opportunities will undoubtedly come to mind. You will also find that some ideas work much better than others, and with experience you will be able to develop a very effective calendar of advertising, sales promotion, and public relations, all working in concert to promote and stimulate your business.

An Important PS: Taglines and Slogans

Taglines and Slogans. It is important to point out that in addition to a mission statement, a vision statement, and a value statement, many companies also develop taglines or slogans, short memorable phrases associated with their companies, to anchor their advertising and communication efforts. While purists claim that technically these two concepts differ, many others contend that taglines and slogans are the same thing and use the terms interchangeably.

For the record, the purists say the difference is that the **tagline**, which is created to catch the essence of what a company does, as well as its personality and positioning, rarely changes in the life of a company. The **slogan**, on the other hand, is a catchy memorable phrase often devised for a specific advertising campaign that tries to create an emotion and is not necessarily specific to the company's business. Despite this distinction, they often overlap, and both are always used to deliver a message that is memorable and recognizable about the company or its products.

While it is not crucial in the beginning stages of a business, as you grow and do more advertising and promotion, the more important a memorable line or slogan/tagline for your business will become. Actually, the sooner you can develop one, the better; it can be an enormous help in developing recognition for your business. You will use it appropriately on all your printed material, and your customers will begin to recognize it and identify your business instantaneously.

Great Slogans and Taglines. These usually have several things in common. They reflect your mission, differentiate you from your competitors, and promise to fulfill a need or desire. They are simple, short, and memorable.

They take time and a great deal of thought to develop. Studying the great ones and looking at your competitors is a great way to start. Then you have to decide how you want to define your business's objectives, how you will deliver them, and what positive effects that will have on your target audience. Next, you should list as many words and phrases as you can to describe your business. Then you have to craft your concepts (or get a wordsmith to) before trying the best candidates on people whose opinions you respect to see if any fly. They may all fail the test, and then it's back to the drawing board. Creating one is not easy, but a great slogan or tagline properly used can help you enormously in achieving your mission and should be worth every bit of the effort you put into developing it.

I had done retail advertising for many years but had never realized the power of a really good slogan until I opened a retail start-up many years ago. My partner and I raised a substantial amount of venture-capital money and opened a 120,000-square-foot lifestyle store called HØME in a suburb of Chicago. Everything was stocked—ready-to-assemble furniture, mostly all imported from Scandinavia, as well as coordinating home furnishings and accessories—all targeted at young consumers just starting out.

Although we had limited advertising funds, we hired a brilliant young advertising agency from New York that designed an unbelievable opening campaign for us. They secured the rights for TV and print to use Judy Garland in *The Wizard of Oz* wearing her magic red slippers, clicking her feet together and saying, "There's no place like home; there's no place like home ..." The campaign was an amazing success. With Judy Garland and the Wizard of

Oz it was instantly recognizable, appealing, and memorable. On opening day we had such a large crowd that the cars were backed up six miles on the major highway leading from downtown to our store. There has never been a question in my mind but that we had Judy Garland and her words, "There's no place like home" (which became our slogan) to thank for our success—or perhaps our advertising agency, which thought of using her.

Many slogans do a wonderful job of expressing their companies' unique selling propositions and become so famous, sometimes lasting for decades, that the minute you hear them you know the company. Some of my favorites are the following:

- I can't believe I ate the whole thing. (Alka-Seltzer)
- You're in good hands with Allstate. (Allstate Insurance)
- Don't leave home without it. (American Express)
- We try harder. (Avis)
- The quicker picker-upper. (Bounty)
- Got Milk? (California Milk Processor Board)
- Does she or doesn't she? (Clairol)
- The pause that refreshes. (Coca-Cola)
- Look, Ma, no cavities! (Crest)
- A diamond is forever. (DeBeers)
- Say it with flowers. (FTD)
- Leave the driving to us. (Greyhound)
- When you care enough to send the very best. (Hallmark)
- 57 Varieties. (H. J. Heinz)
- Finger-lickin' good! (Kentucky Fried Chicken)
- Betcha can't eat just one. (Lay's Potato Chips)
- Because I'm worth it. (L'Oreal)
- Good to the last drop. (Maxwell House)
- Melts in your mouth, not in your hands. (M&Ms)
- When it rains, it pours. (Morton Salt)
- All the news that's fit to print. (*New York Times*)
- With a name like Smucker's, it has to be good. (Smucker's)
- Expect more. Pay less. (Target)

- Where's the beef? (Wendy's)
- The breakfast of champions. (Wheaties)
- Let your fingers do the walking. (Yellow Pages)

The life span of some of these slogans/taglines is truly amazing. The *New York Times* slogan, "All the news that's fit to print," which is still in use, dates back to before 1900!

It is important to note that even though the longer a company uses its slogan the more it has invested in it and the more recognizable it will become to their customers, these taglines and slogans often do change and evolve over time.

If you want some fun, visit Eric Swartz's website (http://www.taglineguru.com),[31] which lists hundreds of the most famous slogans, including those listed above.

---

31 Eric Swartz, "Slogan & Jingle List," *Tagline Guru,* http://www.taglineguru.com/sloganlist.html (accessed October 19, 2011).

CHAPTER 12

Utilizing Internet Marketing

The Internet is undoubtedly the fastest growing of all the communications media and cuts across all marketing disciplines that have just been discussed: advertising, promotion, and public relations. Internet marketing, web marketing, or online marketing is simply using the World Wide Web to offer goods and services. Since more than 78.2 percent of the US population (as of June 2011) is on the Internet,[32] it has drastically changed the very way we approach marketing.

Since the Internet is virtually free and can be accessed from almost anywhere, provided one has a web-enabled device, its power and potential for building brands and customers cannot be ignored. Online marketing offers many tools, such as websites, e-mail capability, social media, blogs, and search engines, as well as the more traditional advertising tools, that can work for any size or type of business. Furthermore, since there are so many viable free or inexpensive ways to reach your potential customers, much of

---

32 "Top 20 Countries with the Highest Number of Internet Users," *Internet World Stats,* http://www.internetworldstats.com/top20.htm (accessed April 23, 2012).

which can also be interactive, web marketing can level the playing field with the big guys for getting the word out.

While many retailers today have founded their businesses solely on the Internet, since the scope of this book is brick-and-mortar retailers, my comments will be confined to briefly discussing how traditional retailers can use the web to market their businesses and increase their chances of success. I must also say that the marketing techniques and opportunities on the Internet are changing so rapidly that I do fear that my remarks, made in March 2012, will be obsolete in the very near future, but I cannot ignore the subject.

For more background and in-depth information, there are many fine books today that cover Internet marketing in great detail. *The McGraw-Hill 36-Hour Course*: *Online Marketing* by Lorrie Thomas is outstanding, as it helps the reader think his or her way through the whole process. And *Web Marketing All-in-One For Dummies* by John Arnold, Ian Lurie, Marty Dickinson, Elizabeth Marsten, and Michael Becker is eight books in one (almost nine hundred pages) and should answer most questions you might have on the subject.

Your Website

Just about anyone in business today needs to have a website to communicate with his or her customers. It can be as simple as a one-pager telling who you are and what your store is all about, or multiple pages containing all sorts of articles and news about your products, advertising special sales, or selling your products directly to your customers. Your website can be as involved as the time you or your designee have to keep it up, because a stale or outdated website is probably much worse than none at all.

Your Website Goals. If you don't already have one, there are many ways to go about creating a website—from doing it yourself to contracting the whole job out—and the resources available today are virtually limitless. To help with this decision you have to first decide specifically what role you want your website to play:

- create or build brand awareness
- provide product or service information
- acquire new customers
- position you as an expert
- make direct sales
- develop a global presence

A good way to begin the process is to review your competitors' websites to get a feeling of how they are using theirs and what they are saying.

In thinking about your goals, consider a longer time horizon than just your immediate needs. Most advise that you should start small and grow your website over time, but it is important when you begin to build it to have an idea of where it may lead so as not to have to redo a lot later on.

Painting with a broad brush, there are generally three types of websites. The simplest is usually a few pages meant to communicate information about your business. The second, more involved and using more technology, adds more character and pizzazz to your website, increasing its appeal. The last is an e-commerce website that allows your customers to make purchases over the Internet.

No matter who develops your website, before you begin you should put together some basic information, which will clarify your thoughts and be invaluable in getting the end result you want from whomever you choose to create it. Describe your company, its history, and its products, as well as your target audience, complete with demographics. Outline and describe your closest competitors. List the goals for your website, being quite specific with an appropriate timetable and budget. Explain what part you envision your website playing in your total marketing effort. (Many advise it should be no more than 10 percent of your marketing plan.)

Ways to Develop a Website. Lots of companies are available on the web to provide all the professional help that you may need, from design companies and webmasters who will do the whole job, to professionals who will help with any area of the process with which you need help.

On one end of the spectrum, having a website developer create a truly **custom-made** one can result in a very original website. But it can be an expensive proposition, costing thousands of dollars, and can take a long time. To avoid disappointment you should know very specifically at the outset what you want when it is completed.

On the other end, web template companies offer templates that can be customized cheaply and quickly. These templates use your own material and allow modifications. Just search the Internet for "website templates," and you will find a limitless supply from which to choose, with prices ranging from free to hundreds of dollars. While some think the finished product using this method can be somewhat stilted and generic, others swear this is the best way for a newcomer to get a functioning website virtually overnight. If originality is important to you, though, you have to be aware that the templates can be sold over and over again and you can run the risk of sameness.

If this will be your first website, perhaps the middle ground, which is easy and usually economical, is the best: selecting a **web hosting company** that offers free website builders, which include not only templates for creating the website, but also other tools and services like helping you get a domain and using designers to customize the templates to whatever degree necessary to satisfy your needs and provide some individuality. Your web host can deliver excellent customer support, even marketing your website to get it out there, and it will provide the web space to support and maintain the content of your site for a modest monthly charge.

In selecting a host to help you build your site, you must focus on your needs and their capabilities, which vary tremendously from the ability to produce simple sites to very complex ones. Obviously, if you are planning e-commerce, you need a more complex site with more tools than if you want to build a simple website just introducing and describing your business to customers.

There are a number of websites that review the top hosting companies in depth, which will help you find the host that is most compatible with your needs. For example, 2012 Best Web Hosting Services (http://www.consumer-rankings.com/hosting/), with a focus on personal and small-business sites, reviews and ranks the top ten hosts; lists monthly costs, amounts of bandwidth, and disc space; gives ease of use and customer support information; and provides links to each host website.

Your Domain Name. Before beginning development on your website, you must select your domain name. Also known as the URL, it is simply the address of your website, but it can play a big part in the ultimate success of your site, depending on how memorable, searchable, or appealing it is. In selecting your domain name, most advise that if you can, you should find one that your customers could guess because it is either the name, or closely related to the name, of your business or expresses the company's core value(s). If your name is shorter and simpler, it is probably easy to remember, and that should cut down on misspellings. Or, if it is simply intriguing, like "Google," a name can be a great asset and draw to the site.

Domain registrars like GoDaddy.com and Register.com (also major web host companies) will do a search on the name(s) you are interested in to see what is available and then, for a nominal fee, register the name for you.

Maintain Control. Just about anyone advising you about your website will caution you to control it from the beginning. You never know what the future will bring, so it is important that, at an absolute minimum, you maintain the original website design files, backups of all content, and control of your domain name and critical logins.

Web Analytics. After your website is up and running for a while, you should definitely consider using web analytics to measure its performance. As Lorrie Thomas says, "While *web analytics* may sound techy and complicated, in reality it is a single line of code you paste into your website's source code to track use and behavior on web pages. The whole operation … can usually be completed in under five minutes. … This line of code will change your web marketing life forever."[33]

This is an amazing tool that allows you to understand and analyze how your customers find you, how they navigate your site, where on your site they spend their time, and what they look at. Studying the results should help you improve the effectiveness of your site by revealing the areas that need improvement, like design flaws that impact or limit your site's use, or the realization that your messages themselves need to be reworked to reach your target customers better. By learning what works most effectively on your site, you can work to incorporate more of the same in all your Internet communications.

This tool is offered by lots of firms, but many experts highly recommend Google Analytics as the best. It is easy to install and is free. To understand its mind-boggling scope, you can visit their website (http://www.google.com/analytics/iq.html) and learn how to use it.

Search Engine Optimization (SEO)

SEO is the process of analyzing and constructing web pages and websites to market your business more effectively by gaining exposure through free, natural search listings, referred to as *organic search*. The reason this is so important is that the overwhelming majority of those who use the web also use a search engine to find information, products, or services. Since most people don't go

---

33   Lorie Thomas, *The McGraw-Hill 36-Hour Course: Online Marketing* (New York: McGraw Hill, 2011), 119.

much beyond the first page of results in their search, the goal is to have your website on that first page.

The major search engines, like Google, Bing, and Yahoo!, use software programs (known as spiders) that "crawl" web pages, follow links from one to another, and index all the content by keywords or phrases to be stored in a gigantic database and later retrieved in searches. These sites or web pages (both new and updated) are added to their index for free. The key, therefore, to optimizing these organic listings is to understand the keywords or phrases that your target audience searches and then utilize those keywords appropriately, not only on your website, but in your other social media as well. In addition, natural links from other websites to your site increase your visibility with the search engines.

If you have professionals build your website, they should be well versed in search engine optimization and should build your website accordingly. As time goes on, however, you will need to either learn how to keep it up yourself or get help from a webmaster or one of the many companies and consultants that offer this service. Like with everything else, some SEO providers are much better and more ethical than others, so any that you select should be carefully referenced.

If you didn't use professionals and your website is up and running, you should, as previously mentioned, have web analytics installed, which will make it easy to pick out the best keywords, some of which may surprise you. You will be able to determine not only which words resulted in the most traffic, but also which converted better into leads and sales. Another way is to look at competitors' websites and find the common key phrases that they use. Finally, there are other options online, like Google's AdWords Keyword Tool, to help you find the most appropriate keywords for your business.

While finding these key phrases is relatively simple, further maximizing your site's visibility by the search engines among the millions of websites out there is not. It is the stuff about which whole books are written. To get a real feel for the scope of this subject, I suggest you google "search engine optimization starter guide by Google," where you will find a wealth of information on SEO, including Google's mind-boggling thirty-two-page guide to search engine optimization.

Finally, as was previously mentioned, a lot of help is available on the Internet to aid you with search engine optimization. For example, one SEO provider, register.com, spells out four alternative programs designed to fit virtually every need and budget. The first, basically a do-it-yourselfer, is priced at $20 monthly and provides the basic tools to improve your site's use of keywords; the next step up, for $25 per month, offers the ability to track links and measure your performance against competitors; the third option, priced at $49.97, includes consulting; and the company's full-service SEO ($300 per month) turns the entire project of site optimization over to register.com consultants.[34]

In addition to organic or free search engine optimization, the next step is paid search and text advertising, which uses the same keyword and phrase technology to help maximize your site's visibility.

Search Engine Marketing/ Pay-Per-Click Ads

One of the big advantages of search engine marketing and advertising is that both can be done very cost-effectively and monitored accurately for their effectiveness and return on investment. However, it is a very complex area and should not be entered into lightly or without a plan.

Although there are many choices for online advertising, by far the greatest dollars are spent on search engine marketing (SEM) because not only is it easy to target campaigns around frequently used phrases that qualify the customer, but there is also tremendous flexibility in where and when the campaigns are run. In addition,

---

34 "Drive Traffic to Your Site with Search Engine Optimization," *Register.com*, http://www.register.com/product/webpromotionmarketing. rcmx (accessed February 10, 2012).

they are extremely cost-effective, since the advertiser only pays when someone clicks on the ad.

Pay-Per-Click Text Ads (PPC). The largest SEM vendors are Google AdWords, Yahoo! Search Marketing, and Microsoft adCenter (Bing), which account for over 90 percent of the market. They sell ads that use keywords/phrases in these pay-per-click text ads, which can also be targeted finely for maximum efficiency. For example, they can be localized by adding the locale to the phrase that is being searched so that they reach only the customers in one's area who are likely to respond and can be serviced, which obviously cuts down on unproductive clicks and saves ad dollars. The ads can be targeted by category, demographics, even zip code, and stopped when the allotted funds are exhausted.

These ads will be ranked and displayed in the "sponsor links" section of the search engine's search results either above or to the right of the normal listings. The cost of the ad varies depending on a number of factors, including the search engine, your business, and the keywords you want to buy.

The cost per click is determined in one of two ways. Either it is based on a flat rate using the factors previously mentioned, or it is bid based, in which case you participate in an auction bidding against others with what you are willing to pay for each click—the higher your bid, the higher your ad will appear on the search results.

Finally, while there are any number of ways of placing these ads and monitoring them, by using Google AdWords, these ads can gain great exposure on appropriate high-profile websites in Google's domain, and the performance can be easily tracked via Google Analytics.

Banner Advertising

Currently banner ads are the second most popular form of online advertising. They are used to promote a website or online company by displaying ads, often colorful or animated to catch attention, across the top of the page or down the side on another website with a link to yours. You can advertise on search engines and directories or run your banner on high-traffic websites or those targeted to specific audiences. And there are a number of exchanges (e.g., http://www.link-exchange.ws) that can help you set up exchanges between your website and others with related content. The technology has advanced to give you, the advertiser, the ability to custom-select not only the website, but also the specific website pages that are most compatible with the product you are advertising.

The cost varies substantially depending on the sites involved, the level of traffic they receive, and also the costing method: by click; per 1,000 views; per lead; or completed sale. For a company that is just starting out, cost-per-click is the method usually recommended.

Many advertisers create their own banner ads that work just fine. There are also many ad agencies and freelance designers that will produce a professional banner with all the bells and whistles for varying costs. Just check the web, and you'll find a multitude.

E-mail Marketing

One of the fastest-growing areas of Internet marketing is e-mail marketing, which has enormous flexibility and can work extremely well despite the tremendous competition for the inbox. E-mail marketing helps you communicate with, collect feedback from, and increase awareness with your customers. In several recent surveys among business executives, e-mail marketing ranked right behind search engine marketing in overall effectiveness. While websites, blogs, and social media have few regulations, e-mails are highly regulated, so you have to be aware of the rules before beginning to play this game.

CAN-SPAM Act. E-mails can be used very effectively in business, but the first thing to understand is that you cannot just write a sales pitch and send it indiscriminately to everyone on an e-mail list. This is considered spam (unsolicited commercial bulk mail).

Commercial messages are controlled by the CAN-SPAM Act (Controlling the Assault of Non-Solicited Pornography and Marketing), which is a compliance guide for businesses written in 2003 and updated in 2008. It spells out the rules and regulations for commercial e-mails, gives individuals the right to stop receiving e-mails, and specifies the penalties for violations, which can be both criminal and financial. For example, a penalty of $16,000 per e-mail in violation can be levied.

It is essential to note that these rules apply only to **commercial messages that are promotional in nature**, not transactional or relationship ones (confirming an already completed commercial transaction, giving information regarding an ongoing commercial relationship like a change of terms, giving warranty or recall information about a product, etc.) *Web Marketing for Dummies* describes the distinction this way: "A commercial e-mail is basically an advertisement, promotion, or content from a business' Web Site. A transactional or relationship e-mail is basically anything other than a commercial e-mail."[35]

The act has several main points: Don't use misleading headers or subject lines. Advise the recipients that the e-mail is an ad. Tell recipients where you are located. Clearly inform them how to simply (by one click) opt out of future e-mails, and honor these requests promptly (within ten days). Manage and monitor everyone sending your e-mails to ensure their compliance with the act. For the full details, see the FTC's detailed explanation "CAN-SPAM Act: A Compliance Guide for Business" on the FTC website (http://www.business.ftc.gov/documents/bus61-can-spam-act-compliance-guide-business). This not only spells out the details of the act, but also includes lots of questions from businesses (with their answers) regarding the act, which clarifies a great deal. Still, when in doubt concerning the act, you should consult your lawyer.

---

35   John Arnold, et al., "Complying with Spam Laws." *Web Marketing for Dummies* (Hoboken, NJ: Wiley Publishing, 2009), 454.

While the act does not require permission up front for the first e-mail, the experts advise that to improve deliverability and readability you should add another step to your compliance in which you receive permission from all recipients before you send your e-mail. (In Canada and most of Europe, receiving permission before sending the initial e-mail is a firm requirement.)

There are several ways to receive permission, but the most common acceptable permission is an **explicit** sign-up or specific opt-in procedure. Systems that automatically sign up a customer, even if it is clearly stated that this is what occurs, pose the issue that the subscriber may well not notice or recall this when the first e-mail arrives and may then label it spam. **Implied permission** (i.e., someone giving you his or her e-mail address in the course of business) isn't really adequate. The best of all is **confirmed permission,** sometimes called double opt-in, by which you send an e-mail back confirming the explicit sign-up or opt-in.

Creating a Successful E-mail Program. There are several steps to creating a successful e-mail marketing campaign.

Creating your mailing list is the first requirement of a successful EM campaign. Rather than just inputting e-mail addresses into your computer, you should buy a separate e-mail program or start with an e-mail service provider's database program to compile your mailing list names (to be discussed further shortly).

While you can build your lists with a list broker or rent lists, this is not the best way, as the quality of the names can be in question, as well as whether they have truly given any kind of permission. By far the most effective lists are usually those that you collect yourself from your own customers. Although it does take time, there are lots of ways to do this. Shopkeepers often place a guest book in their stores or post sign-up links on their websites and every piece of web communication they send. They may also place opt-in forms on ads, in marketing materials, and in social media—often including an incentive or gift for signing up.

Developing your e-mail marketing plan, as with any other marketing effort, is required to reach optimum effectiveness. As a prelude to making this plan, you should conduct a thorough analysis of your competitors' e-mail campaigns (by signing up for their e-mails) to determine their content, strengths, weaknesses, and opportunities.

Next, you need to review your target audience and decide what you want to say to them. What are the goals, being as specific as you can, for your campaign (again by targeted customer type): brand awareness, customer loyalty, sales, traffic, leads, or other targets?

The amount of funds you want to devote to e-mails will help determine how you should proceed in developing your program. By far the most affordable method (other than trying to do it yourself) is to use an e-mail service provider (ESP).

Working with an e-mail service provider is highly recommended if you are planning to use e-mail as a serious marketing tool for your business. Constant Contact and Vertical Response are two well-known ESPs. They can help with database and list management; message creation; deliverability; tracking; and so on.

Your ESP will not only send your e-mails for you (for a monthly fee) but will also provide e-mail templates for you that are easy for you to customize. You can choose from HTML templates that allow you to send e-mails that are more striking than plain text ones. They can include color, bold and italic fonts, and more. While there may be a small setup fee, you save the copywriting, design, and programming fees, which can be hundreds or even thousands per page per e-mail. Your ESP will also be able to provide regrouping of your lists, links to your social media pages, and most important, tracking and analysis of your e-mails for refining your campaign.

They will keep your marketing compliant (most will require that you have received permission to send the e-mails), and they will give your business a professional air. For a comparison of the top sixteen e-mail marketing service providers, check out Top Ten

Reviews' website (http://www.email-marketing-service-review. toptenreviews.com).

Making your e-mails effective is the final step in the process. If you are already sending e-mails, or are preparing to, there are lots of ways to make your e-mails more compelling. Some basic tips are listed below:

- Create a warm and conversational but professional tone.
- Personalize e-mails by greeting each recipient by name.
- Keep your communications simple, short, and clear, with one main message.
- Make your subject line and any headlines enticing.
- Ensure that your "from" line is recognizable to your recipient.
- Make sure your e-mails are relevant to the recipients.
- Include a call to action.
- End with a warm closure and signature line.
- Be sure to include your opt-out information at the end.
- Make sure you (or someone else) has carefully proofread each e-mail.
- Track and analyze your e-mails to continually refine them.

Blogging

One of the newest forms of Internet marketing (around only since the 1990s), blogging has become a powerhouse for those who know how to use it effectively. It is estimated that in 2011 somewhere between 100 million and more than 150 million blogs existed. The biggest blog architect, WordPress, claimed to host 402,328 bloggers on February 2, 2012 (http://www.wordpress. com) and is growing every day.

What Is a Blog? A blog (short for *web log* or *weblog*) is a kind of website that consists of a log of entries or posts in reverse chronological order that presents an ongoing journal of information on just about any subject. Most blogs provide readers with the opportunity to leave comments on the content. When used in a business, it is either part of the company website or linked to it.

Blogs are often used to periodically refresh websites, to increase credentials or branding, and to drive traffic to sites, because search engines, in their quest for fresh information, usually give blogs higher priority. Blogs can disseminate your press releases or news, troll for press coverage with timely articles, help with customer service, and even provide marketing research by eliciting responses to your entries. But perhaps best of all, blogging can build new relationships and project your expertise, and as Lorrie Thomas says in her excellent chapter on the subject, "blogging gives the organization a human face."[36]

Keys to Success. The best business blogs give their readers good, interesting content in a clear, conversational voice. How-to or educational pieces are exceptionally effective in promoting professionalism and brand building. These blogs are often short and simple, but contain the key phrases applicable to their businesses, those that are most sought by the search engines. Frequency, freshness, and timeliness are also important. Many create links to other blogs, sometimes through widgets, small lines of code that permit an interactive experience with your or other websites like social media sites; or companies may embed videos from YouTube or similar sites for added interest.

How to Create a Blog. Although you can host a blog on your own website under your domain name, many prefer to use one of the more preeminent free blog sites like Blogger or WordPress. There are two schools of thought here. The advantage of the free blog sites over your own domain is that you can launch a blog with the

---

36 Lorrie Thomas, *The McGraw-Hill 36-Hour Course*, 73.

free blog site very quickly, in a matter of minutes, and the sites are very easy to use. The disadvantages are that the URL must contain the name of the free blog site; your blog does not reside on your site, so the blog host is in control; and the templates can be constricting. So the choice is yours. As the old proverb goes, "Whoever pays the piper calls the tune."

Social Networking

What Is Social Networking? Social networking is simply the process of interacting with others through websites to share, proliferate, or discuss information using text, pictures, audio, or even video. Social media allow you to profile yourself, make friends, join groups of people with similar interests, converse, collaborate, and even blog.

Merriam-Webster's Eleventh Collegiate Dictionary defines *social media* as "forms of electronic communication (as Web sites for social networking and microblogging) through which users create online communities to share information, ideas, personal messages and other content (as videos)."

Social networking is a tremendous boon to you as an independent shopkeeper. Social media give you a voice to communicate to and interact with your peers, customers, and potential customers in a relaxed, informal way. It allows you to put a face and personality to your company and your brand, and it brings you, your products, and your services alive to your recipients.

Onlineschools.org, which has an interesting infographic worth reviewing, chronicles the history of social networking, beginning with the first e-mail sent in 1971, moving from there up through the development of the earliest social networking sites of the 1990s and Facebook's birth at Harvard in 2004 and its eventual dominance over MySpace as the biggest social networking site in 2008.[37]

---

37   Online Schools, "The History of Social Networking," *Online Schools,* http://www.onlineschools.org/blog/history-of-social-networking/ (accessed April 21, 2012).

Connecting via social networks by individuals for fun and businesses to promote their enterprises is gaining incredible momentum, especially since users can access sites virtually immediately and from anywhere on today's small handheld electronic devices. As of December 2011 Facebook had 845 million monthly users.[38]

There are so many opportunities now, and more keep evolving every day. As usual, books and the web itself are tremendous sources of information and how-to tips. However, as a testament to how complex and how important social media marketing has become, there are any number of adult education courses offered to help one maximize the opportunities. For example, the catalog for the fall 2012 semester at a college near me, Bergen Community College, offers a "Certificate in Social Media for Business"; the completion of five courses covers sixteen full-evening sessions.

The first course is an introduction to social media; it concentrates on how to best use Facebook, Twitter, LinkedIn, YouTube, and blogging in business and what one could expect to achieve by choosing the right ones. The second course focuses on strategy, explores the internal issues that a company will confront when starting a social media program, and helps the class participants create social media marketing plans for their companies. Course three concentrates on how to implement the plan, while the next hones in on the basics of successful blogging. The last course covers how to use mobile phones and location-based services to promote one's business.[39]

Courses like these might well be a worthwhile investment for interested independent business owners. In addition, there are many formal courses and articles on the web to help people gain an understanding of this complex and ever-changing marketing tool.

38   Facebook, "Newsroom: Fact Sheet, Statistics," *Facebook.com*, http://www.newsroom.fb.com/content/default.aspx?NewsAreaId=22 (accessed April 21, 2012).

39   "Business & Industry: Certificate in Social Media for Business," *Bergen Community College*, http://www.bergen.edu/Documents/CE/pdf/Business_and_Industry.pdf (accessed April 21, 2012).

Your Social Networking Plan. While social networking can become a vital marketing tool, it should not be your only Internet effort (as its first purpose is to create awareness); rather it should be integrated into your overall Internet marketing plan. In order to maximize the potential of this valuable tool, you (or someone you designate) must understand how to use it, which sites are most appropriate, and how to monitor them, and then must develop a plan. Remember, however, that building a presence in social media requires patience and does not happen overnight. This is not a quick fix. Most Internet marketers advise that if you can't spend the time to do all that is required to build the relationships, you should find someone who can or just not bother at all.

There are many social media marketers who are very professional and will gladly undertake the activity for you. The only caution is that since you are trusting your company's character to them, you should be sure you do your homework before selecting one. There are tools you can use to check them out, such as Facebook Grader or Twitter Grader. You should assess the agency's own social media campaign; interview their current clients to understand the breadth of their campaigns and their success stories; and be sure that they will start with you by developing an appropriate marketing plan for your company that adequately reflects your goals.

Social Networking Sites. As was posted in *Technology* on August 1, 2011, there are over two hundred networking sites on the web,[40] which fall into different categories or purposes like communication, collaboration, and multimedia. Googling "top social networking websites" will give you a tremendous list of them, including their strengths and weaknesses. The list is so extensive that I will mention just the top few of the moment.

Facebook, as was already mentioned, is the largest social networking site, and it is free. While Facebook builds relationships

40 "How Many Social Networking Websites Are There?" *Technology 1 Aug. 2011*, http://www.howmanyarethere.net/how-many-social-networking-websites-are-there/ (accessed April 21, 2012).

like other sites, it is usually the first choice for business. It delivers results and builds brands and sales through awareness, disseminating information, and providing a two-way conversation between the consumer and the seller in real time. It brings people together, can serve as a very affordable customer-service option, and can give your business a competitive edge. Facebook also offers a cost-per-click advertising option through which your ad can be targeted to a given city, preferred customer age, and specified interest group, so it can be very cost-effective.

Facebook is simple, gives you the option to control what others see, and is constantly evolving to make your experience even more productive and gratifying. Numerous free videos on the web can show you how to get started and use Facebook for an array of purposes.

Twitter is a free social networking platform that allows you to send and receive short messages (140 characters or less) called tweets. It started with the idea of friends/associates telling what they were doing in a sort of microblog in real time, a sort of social messaging. However, it has developed into one of the top social networks, providing news, trends, messages, and more. According to Twitter's blog, as of March 21, 2012, there were 140 million active users sending 340 million tweets a day.[41]

Twitter, founded six years ago by Jack Dorsey, is many different things for both personal and business use. As defined by About. com, "Twitter is micro-blogging. It is social messaging. It is an event coordinator, a business tool, a news reporting service and a marketing utility."[42]

Twitter connects businesses to their customers to build relationships and brands, share information about their products,

41   Twitter, "Twitter turns six, Wednesday, March 21, 2012." *Twitter Blog,* http://blog.twitter.com/2012/03/twitter-turns-six.html (accessed April 22, 2012).

42   Daniel Nations, "What is Twitter?" *About.com. Web Trends,* http:// www.webtrends.about.com/od/socialnetworking/a/what-is-twitter.html (accessed April 22, 2012).

ask market research questions, answer customer-service questions, and check on what competitors are doing, along with a wealth of other things. Like Facebook, there is considerable flexibility as to what can be kept private or made public. You can add photos and updates from your Internet-enabled phone and set up links to other social networking sites, which will be updated instantly. Twitter accounts are powerful in that they are often among the top listings in Google searches.

For an independent retailer with limited ad funds, Twitter can serve as your most valuable promotional tool in communicating, researching, and delivering great customer service. As with Facebook, there are many articles and videos, several from Twitter. com, to help you get started and maximize the flexibility of this fine marketing tool.

LinkedIn is the world's largest professional network, with over 120 million members.[43] As is explained in their excellent website, LinkedIn is a totally business-focused site, which connects you with your contacts to help you keep in touch and exchange ideas, knowledge, and opportunities with an even broader group of professionals in your business. LinkedIn helps you control your online identity, because your professional profile, a sort of resume, usually comes up first on a Google search, which can also be most helpful in attracting new contacts or job opportunities. LinkedIn helps you develop new connections, explore opportunities, and join groups of professionals in your business who discuss issues and solve problems common to your business. You can link to Twitter and stay current using your mobile devices.

YouTube is a free video-sharing website founded in 2005 that allows anyone to share videos with others by uploading, downloading, or commenting on them. You can put just about anything on YouTube, and you can find and watch just about anything on it by searching for the keywords, phrases, or interests of your choice.

---

43   LinkedIn, "What is LinkedIn?" *LinkedIn Learning Center,* http://learn.linkedin.com/what-is- linkedin/ (accessed May 5, 2012).

According to Chad Hurley, cofounder and CEO, YouTube "set out to create a place where anyone with a video camera and an Internet connection could share a story with the world."[44] Few realize just how successful they have been. YouTube delivers two out of every five videos that are viewed online around the world. As an example, this amounted to over 85 billion sent in October 2011.[45]

It is a tremendous and cost-effective marketing tool for business. You can make very professional-looking videos that you can share via e-mail or your social networks, or blog directly from the video page. You can also advertise directly on YouTube.

You can use YouTube to market your company, products, and customer services; share knowledge; and exhibit your expertise. You can create a dedicated channel for the videos that you make and any others that you upload because they are germane to your business. You can include videos explaining your products or services and how-tos to help customers use them; introduce your staff and show your offices; promote events; include customer testimonials; post solutions to common problems; and a host of other things. You can even add relevant links to your videos.

Since YouTube is now owned by Google, it comes with some wonderful tools for you to analyze your videos. You can see who is viewing them, but you can also discover how they found them, which is key information that will help you to create more effective videos in the future.

Finally, YouTube makes it easy to get started. Just go to their website (http://www.youtube.com), and you will find all the information you need to get going.

44   Chad Hurley, "YouTube & the Online Video Revolution," *YouTube Blog*, http://youtube-global.blogspot.com/2010/02/youtube-online-video-revolution.html (accessed April 22, 2012).

45   "More than 200 Billion Online Videos Viewed Globally in October," *ComScore Press Release*, http://www.comscore.com/fre/Press_Events/Press_Releases/2011/12/More_then_200_Billion_Online_Videos_Globally_in_October (accessed April 22, 2012).

Some Tips for Social Networking Success. Once you have your goals and expectations defined and you have devised a good plan, there are a few keys to success in social networking:

- Be consistent and devote the necessary time and resources.
- Have patience, as it will take time to build.
- Communicate (this means not only talking but listening and interacting as well).
- Select the appropriate social media websites and understand their culture and rules.
- Deliver something of value and interest in your communications.
- Become an expert and solve problems for your audience.
- Make it fun.
- Use multimedia to make it more interesting.
- Never spam.

Online Public Relations

Online versus Traditional Public Relations. The Internet has changed public relations dramatically. Before, expensive public relations firms were responsible for most of the high-profile PR efforts. Today if you have access to the web, you can do your own PR for free or seek out all kinds of help available at various prices, depending on what level of involvement you want. Online public relations can not only get you in the news, but it can also enhance your search visibility, make your site more interesting, and attract more visitors as well as online conversations to it.

While the basic skills required in getting good PR are similar in both online and offline venues, the focus and many of the tools are different. Online PR focuses on online media and audiences (search engines, blogs, social networks, etc.) rather than traditional offline media (print, radio, TV, etc.). Traditional public relations centers on media relations with the press. With online PR you can reach your audience directly and even have two-way conversations with them. Furthermore, today's journalists often go online to find information, experts, and news, so you can often reach them as well.

Internet PR Tools. There are a number of tools that you can use to construct a potent PR campaign on the Internet.

Your website, which must be constructed with keywords for search engine optimization, is the center of your PR effort. Search engines are constantly on the lookout for new content, whether it be press releases, blogs, or social media updates, all of which you should constantly be adding to your website.

Online press releases through which you can announce all manner of things about your company, from general news to special events or new products and services are, like in traditional PR, a basic tool. They must, however, include your important keywords and phrases and have links back to your website; and in addition to your logo and pictures, they could also contain videos.

Blogs are another important online PR tool, which are easy to start with services like those offered by blogger.com. They are favored by the search engines and are becoming very important to independent businesses.

Online newsletters sent to a group of subscribers are a great vehicle for building customer loyalty, and make great additions to your website.

Writing articles or participating in forums to inform the general population can be prestigious and valuable tools in building your reputation.

Social media websites like Twitter, Facebook, LinkedIn, and YouTube are excellent PR vehicles, which offer the added advantages of permitting two-way conversations between you and your audience.

Online Help. A number of companies are available to help with every aspect of your effort, in order to help you make the most of these opportunities. Googling whatever you need help with will turn up a wealth of websites to fill your needs. There are websites that help specifically with press release submission and placements; others provide writing help or monitoring tools. Others like HARO provide access to editorial calendars and contacts, while others like PRWeb and Vocus offer it all.

To just get an idea of how extensive the available help is, I suggest you visit PRWeb's website. They offer four different packages, from $89 per release to $369 per release. The basic package, for example (as currently discussed on the PRWeb site), provides a press release template; distributes your release to the major search engines; targets five industries and two regions you want to reach; and permanently hosts your release on the PRWeb site. The premium package includes an interactive, web-optimized release; keyword links to your website; image and video capabilities; distribution to the major search engines, online news sites, and premium offline news outlets; and more than 250,000 PRWeb subscribers and 30,000 bloggers and journalists; plus targeted distribution for ten industries and five regions you select and permanent hosting on PRWeb.com. Get the idea?

There is no question but that the Internet has leveled the playing field with the big guys in public relations—and this can be one of the most important weapons in your marketing arsenal.

Summary

The Internet, if properly used, can allow you to develop a very cost-effective total marketing program that can build your brand and awareness of your company, and drive sales as well as the big guys. However, to be successful you must devote the necessary resources, understand the marketing tools, and learn how they can be used. Furthermore, you have to create a serious marketing plan, a plan that also ensures that whichever tools you use will support and reinforce each other. And finally, you have to have patience. Building your company on the Internet takes time and persistence, but the potential rewards are certainly there.

With the Internet, retail marketing will never be the same. As I review this new medium and consider that much of it is nowhere near a decade old, I find the possibilities for the retailer today both endless and thrilling. I cannot help but wonder with anticipation where future advances will take us and what opportunities to help your business will arise.

CHAPTER 13

Using the Profit and Loss Statement

In the next three chapters I will discuss controlling and growing your business using some basic financial tools. While I will touch briefly on the formulas, examples, and how-tos, my main emphasis will be on how to improve each component that you are measuring. This chapter will cover the following:

- **The P&L Statement:** the basic computation and the main elements to improve your overall results.
- **Increasing Gross Margin for Greater Profitability:** defining the elements of gross margin and how to improve them for more profit, including how to increase your markup and use your markdowns wisely.

Defining the Profit and Loss Statement

The purpose of a profit and loss statement, also known as the income statement, is to measure the success of your business; allow you and others to both understand and compare your profitability to that of others; and help you analyze your business to find areas that can be improved to enhance your profitability.

P&Ls for retailers do vary somewhat from those of other businesses, so if you haven't set up your P&L yet, it is important to use an accountant who is familiar with retail accounting. The profit and loss statement is a simple equation, but perhaps the most important one you will need in your business. It is, keeping it simple:

Net Sales – Cost Of Goods Sold = Gross Profit – Operating Expenses = Profit or Loss.

Example:

Net Sales	$300,000
Minus Cost of Goods	$155,000
Equals Gross Profit	$145,000
Minus Expenses	$130,000
Equals Net Profit	$ 15,000

In this case the net profit/income is $15,000, or 5 percent ($15,000 profit divided by $300,000 sales), which is, as was previously mentioned, a good percentage among successful retailers.

Let's look at a hypothetical P&L for Sally and Sam's with $300,000 in sales this year.

SALLY & SAM'S P&L

	$	%
NET SALES	**$300,000**	**100.0%**
- COST OF GOODS	**$155,000**	**51.7%**
= GROSS PROFIT	**$145,000**	**48.3%**
EXPENSES		
PAYROLL	$49,000	16.3%
RENT	$35,000	11.7%
UTILITIES	$4,200	1.4%
TELEPHONE	$1,800	0.6%
INSURANCE	$3,600	1.2%
MAINTENANCE	$1,000	0.3%
SUPPLIES & POSTAGE	$2,000	0.7%
ADVERTISING	$7,000	2.3%
ACCOUNTING/LEGAL	$6,000	2.0%
ADMINISTRATIVE	$8,400	2.8%
LICENSES/INSPECTIONS	$1,000	0.3%
IS—TECHNOLOGY	$4,000	1.3%
INTEREST	$1,000	0.3%
DEPRECIATION	$5,000	1.7%
MISCELLANEOUS	$1,000	0.3%
- TOTAL EXPENSES	**$130,000**	**43.3%**
= NET PROFIT	**$15,000**	**5.0%**

Now let's go line by line:

Net sales is the gross sales minus returns and allowances.

Cost of goods sold is just that, a calculation to arrive at the cost of the merchandise sold to customers. It is the beginning inventory plus purchases (including freight in) minus ending inventory.

Or, to put it another way, it is the invoice cost plus freight of the goods that you have sold with an adjustment for any change in your inventory levels from the beginning of the period to the end of it.

Gross profit is net sales minus the cost of goods sold. This is a very important number because gross profits are the dollars available not only for paying expenses but also for profit. In this example, the net sales ($300,000) minus the cost of goods ($155,000) gives us a gross profit of $145,000. While there is often confusion between the terms *gross profit* and *gross margin* and they are often used interchangeably, to be precise there is a difference.

Gross margin (also sometimes called gross profit margin) is stating the gross profit dollars as a percent of net sales. So, while gross profit is always in dollars, gross margin is typically stated as a percentage. In this case, to determine the gross margin, divide the $145,000 gross profit by the $300,000 net sales; this amounts to a gross margin of 48.3 percent.

Expenses are the bills you pay to run your business, usually known as SG&A (selling, general, and administrative), and this figure includes salaries, rent and utilities, advertising, interest and depreciation, and so on.

Net profit or net income is the funds that remain after all the expenses have been paid at the end of the designated period. Please note that the income taxes a business pays are handled differently depending on the company's legal entity. For example, a C Corporation usually shows the income tax as a separate line item on the P&L, while most other business types, including sole proprietorships, usually do not list tax expenses on the P&L of a retail company.

We can see from the P&L equation that there are just three ways of increasing profit:

- increasing sales (revenue)
- decreasing expenses
- increasing gross margin

All three areas are worthy of continual, or at least periodic, review.

Increasing Revenue or Sales. Previously we have talked a lot about how to increase sales by refining your store's positioning and product offering, increasing customer service, advertising and promotion, and so on. While these all take time, fortunately the benefits are usually long-lasting. In the following gross margin section we will discuss some additional ways.

Decreasing Expenses. This is, of course, an obvious way to increase profits, providing there are expenses you can cut. Unlike increasing sales, where you realize only a percentage of the increase in profits (for the cost of goods and expenses must come out of them), with decreasing expenses you can realize a dollar in profits for each one saved. It stands to reason, therefore, that one of the most important reasons for keeping close track of all expenses is to be able to hold periodic reviews (at least seasonally) of each category to see if there are opportunities for savings.

Just like your own personal expenses, some categories seem to get out of line frequently and need to be policed so they don't continue that trend. It will be most helpful if, through retail organizations you belong to or through your own research, you can learn average expense ratios for your classifications to help direct you to the areas that can probably be reduced without harming your business. While decreasing expenses appropriately is an immediate way to increase your profit, most retailers do concentrate heavily in this area.

Increasing Gross Margin for More Profit. While most retailers spend a lot of effort on increasing sales and cutting expenses, methods for increasing gross margin are not always as clearly understood or maximized. This is a very fertile area for increasing your profits. It can be approached from several different angles, which I will discuss for the balance of this chapter.

Increasing Gross Margin for Greater Profitability

We can increase gross margin by the following methods:

1. Raising retails
2. Lowering the cost of goods
3. Growing the more profitable categories
4. Using markdowns wisely
5. Decreasing markdowns
6. Decreasing shortage

Raising Retails to Increase Markup. The easiest way to increase gross margin is to evaluate the markup of each item, looking for opportunities to raise your initial retails and bearing in mind the following:

Competition. Most importantly, if you have the item alone you can price it, as they say, at whatever you think the traffic will bear. If the product is all over town, however, you'll need to price it somewhere in the prevailing range to avoid developing the stigma of being overpriced.

Brand value. The type of brand will dictate to some degree how high you can go. If it is a high-end brand, you have more leeway than with a commodity-type brand. By the same token, if your operation is upscale, you will have an easier time with slightly higher prices than a more mainstream or discount operation.

Perceived value. How much does the item appear to be worth? If you didn't know the cost (and in most instances your customers surely don't), how much do you believe they would be willing to pay for it?

Using the art of pricing. Price your wares to reflect their overall value within the totality of your retail world. Specialty stores cannot, of course, offer the lowest price around because of the smaller quantities they buy, the higher freight they pay, and the costs of the extra services they offer—nor do their customers expect this. But what customers *do* expect, and what they will respond to, is a consistent pricing policy and a fair price policy, which includes the intrinsic value of the product; the ambience and reputation of the store; and the level of extra services it provides, from sales help (including individual attention) to gift wrap and other amenities.

I was taught a valuable lesson about pricing early in my retailing career when I was the Bath Shop buyer at Bloomingdale's. After I made my first foreign buying trip, my initial imports came in and needed to be priced. Since they were at that time exclusive to my department, due to the simple fact that they were imports, competition around town was a nonissue. To begin the process, my boss took the invoice away from me so I could not see how much the items cost landed (including freight, duty, etc). Instead of focusing on the landed cost and applying a predetermined markup, which as previously mentioned many merchants do, he forced me to decide on the retails just by looking at and touching the items and considering how much they were worth relative to the pricing of similar items already in my assortment. (Obviously if the price of the item makes no sense to a similar one sitting next to it, one of them probably won't sell.) This first invoice came out with a 66 percent markup (three times landed cost), and everything sold without a single markdown!

Pricing this way means, of course, that you work shorter on some items and longer on others, but this method is effective and usually nets a higher overall markup than applying a set percentage. Furthermore, if your pricing makes sense to you, chances are that it will make sense to your customers as well, unless they know something that you don't.

If you are one of the many retailers who use a predetermined pricing grid or markup percent to establish the retail of an item, try this other method on your next shipment of new goods and see how it works for you (remembering, of course, that you have much less leeway on an item that is all over town).

I have found that it is also a good idea to get others' opinions on pricing. Store salespeople can be very helpful in this regard. Your customers will be helpful too, as they will tell you if the price is too high by their lack of interest in an item after being told the price, or by letting the item just sit on the shelf while they buy up the other items around it.

Remember also that how your store looks is a strong factor in influencing how you retail your goods. If you look like a warehouse, you will have difficultly pricing like Tiffany's.

Lowering the Cost of Goods. The second way to increase your gross margin is by finding ways to lower the cost of your goods and services by looking into the feasibility of the following:

- getting a better price from the vendor
- buying in larger quantities to either get a break in the price or lower the freight cost
- participating in a rebate program, if available
- obtaining special discounts or closeouts that you can sell at regular price
- seeking higher-margin goods

Growing the More Profitable Categories. This is another important way to increase your overall margin, which you can accomplish in a number of different ways, including the following:

- enlarging these assortments
- giving them better real estate and perhaps more space
- enhancing the displays, signage, and collateral material

- advertising or promoting them more often
- focusing on an in-stock position of key profitable items. (This is one of the easiest ways to increase gross margin and sales. Many independent retailers make the mistake of waiting until an item is out of stock to reorder it. This is a sure way to lose sales and not maximize the potential of an item or class. Your customers have told you what they like by making them your best sellers, while new products may or may not get the same acceptance.)

Using Markdowns Wisely. Many retailers are reluctant to take markdowns because they think they come right out of their profit. But while they do, the other side of the coin, which should be kept in mind, is that, if managed properly, markdowns can be a valuable tool for increasing gross margin and profits. So let's discuss markdowns in general, looking at both sides of the coin.

There are, of course, two types of markdowns: promotional markdowns used to stimulate sales, and regular or permanent markdowns used to adjust the inventory to a truer market value, or to clear the item perhaps to invest the funds in more salable merchandise.

Promotional markdowns are in effect while the sale or promotion is on, and the item goes back to regular price after the event. Promotional markdowns are a key ingredient to stimulating sales and can be very effective in increasing profits if they are not abused and overused.

Permanent markdowns are used to adjust the price when the merchandise will not be brought back to the original price, and they may often be followed by additional markdowns if the objective is to clear the goods. This is a tool often underused by independent retailers because they may not understand the importance of taking clearance markdowns on a regular basis or when it is time to take them.

How do you know when it is time to take a permanent markdown on regular goods? The rate of sale will tell you. For example, if you bought twelve of an item and at the end of eight weeks you have sold two, you will still have ten left. If you have sold only two in eight weeks, it means you have sold, on average, one a month. If you have ten left, you still have a ten-month supply on hand. If you want to turn your inventory only two times (on average you should be aiming for at least three times), you should have sold four, or two per month—so it is time to begin considering a markdown if sales don't start to pick up.

We all hate to take permanent markdowns, not only because we know it cuts into our profits, but even worse, we have to admit that we were wrong. Our little darlings didn't like what we bought. And we were so sure they would! What is the matter with them anyway? Don't they have any taste?

There are also other very basic reasons that we need to take a permanent markdown:

- overbuying (the item might be right, but we just bought way too many)
- bringing the item in too early, before the customer wanted it
- bringing it in too late, after the season
- having no plan to sell it
- displaying the item poorly
- going back to the well once too often (too many repeat orders on fashion items)
- being undersold by a competitor
- paying too much, which usually translates into retails being too high
- overpricing an item (thinking your customers will pay more for it than they will)
- having broken sizes or assortments
- bringing in items of inferior quality

Bottom line, by using your markdowns wisely, you will increase your gross margin by adding additional sales through promotion;

and through the ability to buy new, fresher, and hopefully more salable, merchandise with the freed-up markdown funds.

Decreasing Markdowns. There are a number of key disciplines and procedures (some already previously alluded to) that will help you decrease your markdowns, obviously increasing both your gross margin and your profitability:

Buy better through learning from your mistakes and understanding better what your customer wants and what he or she is willing to pay for it.

Reevaluate constantly if you should—or how much you should—reorder, or how large the initial buy should be.

Test merchandise whenever feasible.

Reduce the price sufficiently the first time. You have probably heard the saying, "Your first markdown is your best markdown." And that is absolutely right. All too often we are chintzy about taking that first markdown, and the result is that the item continues to sit on the shelf unwanted by anyone. Reduce it enough the first time to get the item to a price where it will sell! The second markdown will probably be much more costly, and your money will be tied up longer than it has to be.

Mark down merchandise on a timely basis, not just at the end of the season. Waiting until the end of the season will undoubtedly cause a much more costly markdown than addressing a slow mover early on and showing the customer a value when he or she really needs or wants it.

To reiterate, it is better to take a 20 percent markdown on slow-moving or overstocked goods a week or more before Christmas than to wait until after Christmas when you have to take at least 50 percent off. Obviously you are also better off taking a markdown when you have a lot of store traffic and the item is wanted, rather than when the season is over and your customers have moved on to other things.

Take seasonal markdowns by the end of the season; and as a general rule, *do not hold goods over from season to season*. Unlike fine wines, merchandise "dogs" seldom get better with age. Believing they do is a mistake that independents often make when they pack up seasonal merchandise (especially Christmas or Easter) and save it for the next year, rather than mark it down to the proper price to clear it during the season for which it has been purchased.

Think if it this way. Holding seasonal merchandise from one season or year to another is the same as buying it again the next year. If it didn't sell through the first year, it probably won't become more desirable by being a year older. In addition, your money is tied up for the whole year when you could use those funds to buy merchandise to sell all year and increase your turnover.

There are, of course, exceptions to this rule, when it does make sense to pack up some merchandise and save it for the following year. Whenever you make that decision, though, be sure that you are not simply taking the easy way out.

Disguise your dogs in a storewide sale, and use them as loss leaders in promoting your business. When you have a storewide sale or a major sale event, take some of your most unwanted goods and really whack the retail. Not only will you probably clear the items, but they can also add a real sense of value, credibility, and excitement to your sale.

Move your markdowns to a special place in the store, and highlight them with special signage to call attention to the fact that they are a special value. Also, individually marking the items with sale prices hitting natural promotional price points is vastly superior to signing the area with a percentage off (other than 50 percent off, which most people can handle calculating). More esoteric amounts, like "1/3 off," are often difficult to figure in one's head and can cause customers to pass right on by.

Ask your vendor for markdown money or return privileges for merchandise that is not moving.

Establish a six-month plan and an open-to-buy system. Finally, if you are not already, begin to work toward planning your buys in accordance with the seasonal flow of your business. These systems will discipline you to buy better. They will prevent you from buying whatever you want, whenever you want, so you will have the funds to bring in merchandise when it is needed to make your sales plan.

Reducing Shortage. The last element in increasing gross margin is reducing shortage. This is so much easier said than done; the key here lies in doing all you can to prevent reductions from bookkeeping errors, credit and check fraud, shoplifting, and employee theft (the largest cause).

With the advent of the new POS (point of sale) and electronic surveillance systems, overall shortage has been reduced, but it still amounts to billions of dollars a year. Reducing shrinkage is not brain surgery, but it involves a great many aspects of your operation and is certainly an area that deserves constant attention to the basics from all your employees. From how you design your store, to utilizing customer-service techniques, to posting policies on shoplifting, to auditing your bookkeeping, to name just a few, this is a very large subject. Fortunately, many books have been written to help you with this task. If you Google "top 10 retail loss prevention books," you will get a flavor of what is available.

When you consider that most stores run a shortage of 1.5 percent to 2 percent or more, wouldn't it be nice to add that amount to your profit, especially since, as we have previously noted, many operations do not even make a 2 percent profit? Now that is something to ponder!

CHAPTER 14

Merchandising Plans: The Six-Month Plan and OTB

The **six-month merchandising plan** and **open-to-buy** are the road maps and the controls for your business. The old saying, "failure to plan is a plan for failure" was never truer than to illustrate the worth of these two practices in retailing. Even though businesses do open and grow without them, I think this is foolhardy if yours is or will be of any significant size; and I can just about guarantee that your growth and ultimate success will be severely curtailed without them. Without these plans/controls, you are like someone setting out on a long trip, only *sort of* knowing where you want to go, but not having a map or navigation system to guide you there.

Your accountant can help you with setting up this process and should also help you find the right registers and software for your business. The key to this planning is to be able to track your inventory and sales by classification or department. If you cannot do that, you cannot do either six-month plans or the open-to-buy calculation.

Depending on the size of your operation, there are many POS systems, management-information systems, and inventory-management/replenishment systems on the market today that can handle this need for you, partially or almost totally automatically. But all will require initial setup assumptions and revisions that you will need to make as your business conditions change—especially before the beginning of each season.

You can, however, also set up Excel spreadsheets yourself, as long as you have the sales and inventory information. The only caution here is that these plans should be done by department and classification, so if you have lots of classifications or departments, it can become quite a task—and with all the automated systems available today, this is hardly as necessary as it once was.

Let us discuss the philosophy and basic how-to behind setting up these financial plans.

Creating the Six-Month Merchandising Plan

The six-month plan is the beginning of the process and is done for each of two seasons—spring, usually from the beginning of February to the end of July; and fall, from the first of August to the end of January. This timing is selected by most retailers (rather than the first and last six months of the calendar year) because it makes more sense to end the retail fiscal year with January than December. Retailers take clearance markdowns as December concludes, many of which are booked in January but rightfully belong in the fall season. Also, most retailers take inventory in January because their stocks are usually at the lowest then, and they normally have the fewest customers in the store during this month.

Many large retailers do both their spring and fall seasonal plans together several months in advance of the new year. In late spring they revise their fall plans, incorporating any new information they may have. These retailers do their six-month plans at the classification level within each department, at the department level, at the division level, and finally, at the store level. I do not think all these levels are necessary for a small store, but I do believe in the value of an overall plan at the total store level and plans by department or major category.

Plans by department are important because each department has a different turnover rate, and carries a different set of products that cannot be interchanged by the customer for those of another. If a customer comes into a store for dinnerware, for example, and the pattern he or she wants is out of stock, he or she will not usually substitute sheets from the bedding department—so each department (or even better, each major category) should be planned and controlled separately. Doing plans by department/classification ensures that you can treat each according to its needs, and it precludes spending too much money on inventory for a department or class where it is not justified.

In addition to sales, markdowns, and inventory, larger retailers also plan and track all aspects of their profitability by month as well. The typical large operation six-month plan consists of the following:

1. Sales
2. Stock levels and stock to sales (turnover)
3. Markdowns
4. Purchases
5. Markup
6. Gross margin

As was already stated, if you are not familiar with the six-month-plan process, you should either purchase a good retail system and/or get someone who is very familiar with the process, like a retail accountant, to help you, since this process can be somewhat formidable, especially in the beginning.

Let's illustrate the thought process behind the six-month plan by creating a fictitious first six-month plan for our retailer, Sally and Sam's. This plan will concentrate on the first four elements (sales, stock levels, markdowns, and purchases). These are the most practical to deal with monthly for an independent; but markup and gross margin should be reviewed formally, at least on a quarterly basis, with constant and ongoing awareness for their improvement.

Please note that, since this is the first plan for Sally and Sam's, each element will be planned from scratch, exhibiting the basic thought process, and shown in our example of the initial year we are planning. If, however, Sally and Sam's had been in business last year, the plan for each of the elements would begin with a line of last year's actual, and would then show the percent change from last year to arrive at this year's plan, before the line indicating this year's plan. In addition, the plan would probably include a markup/margin section. Finally, if this was an actual plan, you would also include a line for each item for this year's actual.

As we begin, it is recommended that all figures used be retail, not cost. The six-month plan can be done at cost, but, since your sales are at retail, this is by far the easier way to go. Above all, *cost figures should never be mixed with retail figures.* The first element in the plan is sales.

Sales. First, you must plan your *net* sales (sales minus returns and allowances) by month. *Of all the items in your plan, this one is the most critical, as it drives all the others.* If the sales forecast is too high, you will end up with extra inventory and a higher accounts payable; too low, and you won't have sufficient inventory, which will ultimately cost you sales. Either will cause your future forecasts to be incorrect. The biggest error that most retailers make is being too optimistic. Young buyers will often plan their sales too aggressively to obtain more open-to-buy, but in this instance it really pays to be as realistic as possible, as inflated sales will only backfire on you and ultimately choke your stocks when they don't happen.

The biggest factors generally in determining the monthly sales flow are the seasonal weather patterns and holidays. Bathing suits obviously sell in the summer and practically not at all in the winter (except in warm climates), whereas sales for most commodities are greater just about everywhere at Christmastime. While each category has its own beat, which will become clear after a few seasons, history is the best forecaster of seasonal and monthly sales for each category.

Many variables also influence future sales projections. For example, a specific weather happening last year, like a big snowstorm three days before Christmas, might have adversely affected the business, but presents an opportunity for greater sales this year because the customers can get to the store. (This is the reason retailers religiously mark their annual calendar with the weather each day.) Or, being understocked in a category last year, but having lots of exciting new merchandise this year, should certainly present an opportunity for greater sales this season. Significant changes in advertising patterns will also greatly affect the sales plan, as will the opening or closing of a competitor.

So, if you have history from the year before, start with these monthly sales and adjust them up or down to reflect whatever you expect in the future months relative to your business trend and the business climate in general.

If you are starting from scratch, take your estimated annual sales and multiply those by the percent per month normally done in this category. (These averages for broad categories can usually be found through the census bureau, through industry associations, or sometimes through particularly knowledgeable vendors.)

Let's take the spring six-month plan for Sally and Sam's step by step. The annual sales plan is $300,000, and for this type of home furnishings store, the listed monthly sales percentages below on Sally and Sam's spring sales chart are fairly common. For February's sales forecast, taking 6.9 percent of the annual $300,000 equals $20,700; 7.9 percent for March equals $23,700, etc.

SALLY & SAM'S SPRING SALES PLAN							
	FEB	MAR	APR	MAY	JUNE	JULY	SEASON
SALES PLAN $	$20,700	$23,700	$21,900	$24,600	$26,100	$25,500	$142,500
PLAN %	6.9%	7.9%	7.3%	8.2%	8.7%	8.5%	47.5%
BOM STOCK							
MARKDOWNS							
PURCHASES							
EOM STOCK							

Beginning-of-Month Inventory. Next, you must plan your inventory levels. While inventory or stock levels are set in a number of different ways, I believe the easiest, especially for those without history, is using the stock-to-sales-ratio method, in which you set a reasonable stock turnover goal for the commodity you are selling—a stock turn that will result in enough inventory to execute the sales plan and ultimately make a profit.

Turnover is how many times a year your average inventory is sold and replaced. For a new business, you will have to research what the average turn is for your kind of business from industry figures or competitors in a similar business. If you are already in business, you have your historical data from last year upon which to build. Obviously the faster the turn, the better, for it means you will have fewer dollars tied up in inventory, but if your turn is too fast, you will starve your inventory and lose sales.

For the many specialty stores and home furnishings businesses within department stores that I've been involved with, stock turns ranged between two and three times a year, while ready ready-to-wear was higher, at 3.5 or four. Other businesses, like fresh-food stores, for example, have very much higher turnover, while an antique store would typically have a much lower turnover—

possibly only one. Average turns by category are available through any number of retail organizations, as well as often though knowledgeable vendors.

If you are already in business, you should base your inventory levels and monthly stock-to-sales ratios on your history, and make appropriate adjustments based on this year's business prospects.

Let us assume you have (like Sally and Sam's), or plan to have, annual net sales of $300,000 and want to turn your inventory three times. Your average monthly inventory will be $100,000 ($300,000 divided by a three-time turn).

Furthermore, if you turn your inventory three times in twelve months, your stock-to-sales ratio becomes 4:1 and your factor becomes four, because twelve months' inventory divided by three turns (which equals four months' supply). Or to say it another way, this factor of four means you will have four months of stock on hand to do one month's sales. So using our example, the beginning-of-month inventory (BOM) for February is February's planned sales of $20,700 times the ratio/factor of four (that is, $82,800); March's is $23,700 multiplied by four ($94,800), and so on, as on Sally and Sam's Spring BOM Stock Plan below.

SALLY & SAM'S SPRING BOM STOCK PLAN							
PLAN $	FEB	MAR	APR	MAY	JUNE	JULY	SEASON
SALES	$20,700	$23,700	$21,900	$24,600	$26,100	$25,500	$142,500
BOM STOCK	$82,800	$94,800	$87,600	$98,400	$104,400	$102,000	
S-to-S Ratio	4	4	4	4	4	4	4
MARKDOWNS							
PURCHASES							
EOM STOCK							

End-of-Month Stocks. Now let's enter these, which is easy because the end-of-month stock is simply the next month's beginning stock, so March's BOM of $94,800 becomes February's EOM; April's BOM of $21,900 becomes March's EOM stock; and so on. (See the spreadsheet below.)

SALLY & SAM'S SPRING EOM STOCK PLAN							
PLAN $	**FEB**	**MAR**	**APR**	**MAY**	**JUNE**	**JULY**	**SEASON**
SALES	$20,700	$23,700	$21,900	$24,600	$26,100	$25,500	$142,500
BOM STOCK	$82,800	$94,800	$87,600	$98,400	$104,400	$102,000	
MARKDOWNS							
PURCHASES							
EOM STOCK	$94,800	$87,600	$98,400	$104,400	$102,000		

To plan July's EOM you have two choices. If you are planning the whole year, or are using last year's figures, you will know what your August BOM should be. If not, average the five preceding months' EOM by totaling them and then divide by five.

$$\$94,800 + \$87,600 + \$98,400 + \$104,400$$
$$+ \$102,000 = \$487,200$$

$$\$487,200 \div 5 \text{ (number of months)} = \$97,440 \text{ (July's EOM)}$$

SALLY & SAM'S SPRING EOM STOCK PLAN COMPLETE							
PLAN $	**FEB**	**MAR**	**APR**	**MAY**	**JUNE**	**JULY**	**SEASON**
SALES	$20,700	$23,700	$21,900	$24,600	$26,100	$25,500	$142,500
BOM STOCK	$82,800	$94,800	$87,600	$98,400	$104,400	$102,000	
MARKDOWNS							
PURCHASES							
EOM STOCK	$94,800	$87,600	$98,400	$104,400	$102,000	$97,440	

Markdowns/Reductions. Next you have to plan your markdown reductions to your stock caused by promotions, slow-selling merchandise or overbuying, damaged or stolen merchandise, and employee discounts. As was mentioned earlier, this is an area where retailers tend to be very conservative, often not wanting to admit their mistakes or the extent of other factors that cause markdowns. I must reiterate that you should be very realistic. Keeping merchandise too long or not taking other markdowns on a timely basis will not only cause greater markdowns later on but may well prevent you from purchasing replenishment goods or newer goods with a greater potential for sales. On the other hand, excessive markdowns the previous year caused, for example, by poor buys offer an opportunity for greater profit this year, but remember to account for a number of goofs this year, too. No one can be right all the time, especially in trying to guess what the customer will like or when exactly he or she might want it!

If you have last year's history, start with those markdown dollars and make any adjustments warranted to forecast how much will be needed for this year. If you have no history, you will use a constant rate monthly, knowing full well that more will be used some months and less other months.

While ready-to-wear retailers often have a markdown rate as high as 25 percent, many other retailers have much lower ones. Since Sally and Sam's is a home furnishings company, we will use a constant 10 percent for markdowns, which will include 2.5 percent for shortage and employee discounts. (Some retailers do not include these in this markdown calculation, but apply them at the end of the period. Applying them here, however, ensures they remain top of mind.)

SALLY & SAM'S SPRING MARKDOWN PLAN							
PLAN $	FEB	MAR	APR	MAY	JUNE	JULY	SEASON
SALES	$20,700	$23,700	$21,900	$24,600	$26,100	$25,500	$142,500
BOM STOCK	$82,800	$94,800	$87,600	$98,400	$104,400	$102,000	
MARKDOWNS	$2,070	$2,370	$2,190	$2,460	$2,610	$2,550	$14,250
	10%	10%	10%	10%	10%	10%	10%
PURCHASES							
EOM STOCK	$94,800	$87,600	$98,400	$104,400	$102,000	$97,440	

Purchases. The purchases for the month are a result of the planned end-of-month stock (which is also, remember, the beginning of the next month's stock) to which are added this month's sales and other reductions (markdowns and shortage) and from which the month's opening inventory is deducted. The formula is as follows:

Purchases = End-of-Month Inventory + Month Sales + Markdowns – Beginning of Month Inventory

Using this formula, the Sally and Sam's purchase plan for February is $34,770:

Feb EOM + Feb sales plan + Feb markdown
plan – Feb BOM = Feb purchases

$94,800 + $20,700 + $2,070 - $82,800 = $34,770

To arrive at the purchase plan for March use this calculation:

Mar EOM + Mar sales plan + Mar markdown
plan – Mar BOM = Mar purchases

$87,600 + $23,700 + $2,370 – $94,800 = $18,870

Use the same method for the balance of the spring season as below.

SALLY & SAM'S SPRING PURCHASE PLAN							
PLAN $	FEB	MAR	APR	MAY	JUNE	JULY	SEASON
SALES	$20,700	$23,700	$21,900	$24,600	$26,100	$25,500	$142,500
BOM STOCK	$82,800	$94,800	$87,600	$98,400	$104,400	$102,000	
MARKDOWNS	$2,070	$2,370	$2,190	$2,460	$2,610	$2,550	$14,250
PURCHASES	$34,770	$18,870	$34,890	$33,060	$26,310	$23,490	$171,390
EOM STOCK	$94,800	$87,600	$98,400	$104,400	$102,000	$97,440	

Sally and Sam's Spring Plan. Now let's review and summarize the total spring plan:

Sales are planned at $142,250, which is 47.5 percent of the annual plan of $300,000, with the fall season being planned as the balance. In our example, historical monthly percentages for a specific home furnishings business have been used. You would use the average percentages for your business category; or if you have sales history, you would use your own history from last year, adjusting each month's forecast up or down depending on your calendar of events and this year's opportunities or shortfalls.

Stocks are planned at a constant factor of four (the stock-to-sales ratio is 4:1), reflecting an annual stock turn of three. Again, if you have history, you would use your stock-to-sales ratio by month for the previous year, making any adjustments necessary, to plan your monthly BOM stocks for this year. Otherwise you would research what is typical turn for your business.

Markdowns have been planned at a constant 10 percent in our example. If you have history, you would use your monthly history from last year and make appropriate adjustments. Otherwise, use a figure that is supported by your research.

Average inventory is $95,349, which you arrive at by adding February's BOM of $82,800 and the EOMs for all six months (equaling $667,440) and then dividing by seven. If you take your sales of $142,500 divided by your average inventory of $95,349, you get a 1.5 season turn. To annualize the season's turn of 1.5, multiply by 2, and you will get your annual stock turn of three. The finished plan look likes this:

SALLY & SAM'S SPRING PLAN							
SPRING SALES	$142,500				SPRING TURN		1.5
MARKDOWNS	10.0%				AVG. STOCK		$95,349
PLAN $	FEB	MAR	APR	MAY	JUNE	JULY	SEASON
SALES	$20,700	$23,700	$21,900	$24,600	$26,100	$25,500	$142,500
BOM STOCK	$82,800	$94,800	$87,600	$98,400	$104,400	$102,000	
MARKDOWNS	$2,070	$2,370	$2,190	$2,460	$2,610	$2,550	$14,250
PURCHASES	$34,770	$18,870	$34,890	$33,060	$26,310	$23,490	$171,390
EOM STOCK	$94,800	$87,600	$98,400	$104,400	$102,000	$97,440	

Using the Open-to-Buy Concept

Open-to-Buy. This is an extremely valuable tool that helps keep your inventory commensurate with your sales plan by detailing how much money you have left to spend monthly after tallying your commitments and reviewing the current state of your business. It is based on the six-month merchandise plan and essentially is a budget corrected on an ongoing basis with all your commitments and deviations from the previous month's plan. While the OTB can be done at cost or retail, overwhelmingly most recommend keeping it at retail, since sales, which drive the whole calculation, are made at retail. (This, of course, means that your purchases must be converted from cost to retail.)

There are many reasons why an open-to-buy system is so important for your business. Not only does it lay out the amount of inventory and stock dollars needed by month to make your sales plan, but it also keeps a good flow of merchandise to your store to keep it fresh, and helps you control and monitor your investment, making the necessary corrections when sales perform differently than your plan.

While numerous software packages and many POS systems include an open-to-buy module, theoretically OTB can be done on an Excel spreadsheet, providing you have the necessary information (but it would be *extremely* time-consuming if you have several categories). By category or department is the best way, but for a new small operation, an OTB at store level can be effective.

The OTB formula is below:

Planned Sales + Planned Markdowns + Planned EOM Inventory – Planned BOM Inventory – On Order = Open-to-Buy

So let's see how it works using our last six-month-plan example:

PLAN $	FEB	MAR	APR	MAY	JUNE	JULY	SEASON
SALLY & SAM'S SIX MONTH PLAN - SPRING SEASON OTB							
SALES PLAN	$20,700	$23,700	$21,900	$24,600	$26,100	$25,500	$142,500
BOM STOCK PLAN	$82,800	$94,800	$87,600	$98,400	$104,400	$102,000	
MARKDOWN PLAN	$2,070	$2,370	$2,190	$2,460	$2,610	$2,550	$14,250
PURCHASE PLAN	$34,770	$18,870	$34,890	$33,060	$26,310	$23,490	$171,390
COMMITMENTS	$31,400	$16,750	$25,671	$12,541	$6,521	$200	$93,083
OPEN-TO-BUY	$3,370	$2,120	$9,219	$20,519	$19,789	$23,290	$78,307
EOM STOCK	$94,800	$87,600	$98,400	$104,400	$102,000	$97,440	

Let's look at the first three months. Assume that we are in the last week of January and you have placed orders for delivery in February ($31,400), March ($16,750), and April ($25,671) against your monthly planned purchases for these months ($34,770, $18,870, $34,890, respectively).

At this point in time you still have $3,370 open-to-buy (money to purchase inventory) left for February; $2,120 for March; and $9,219 for April. That is, your planned purchases for February are $34,770 minus your commitments of $31,400, which leaves $3,370 that you can still spend and receive. March's purchases are planned at $18,870, of which $16,750 has been committed, so only $2,120 OTB for March remains. April's commitments of $25,671 against purchases of $34,890 leave only $9,219 open to spend and receive for April.

I should point out that many think the open-to-buy should be called the open-to-receive, because that is really more accurate. The only purchases that you make for any month that count against that month's open-to-buy are those that will be *received* that month. As an example you could, and probably would, write more orders in February than February's remaining open-to-buy, but their receipts would be in later months and would come off the OTB for those future months. Theoretically, you could place all the orders for the season at the beginning of the season, as long as you scheduled their receipt in conjunction with the purchases allowed each month on your OTB.

Most retailers review updated open-to-buys at least weekly, but at the minimum your open-to-buy for future months must be adjusted at the end of every month based on new orders/commitments you have placed and your actual results for the month against plan.

Any of the planned items that change will change your open-to-buy. If you achieve fewer sales or don't take your full quota of markdowns, you will lose OTB. If you exceed your sales or markdowns, you will have more OTB. If you bring in more merchandise than your plan, you will lose OTB either this month or in the subsequent months.

In this case, for example, at the end of January, January's results against plan will change February's OTB as follows:

- **Sales** over plan will be added to February's OTB; sales under plan will be deducted from February's OTB.
- **Markdowns** over plan will be added to February's OTB; markdowns under plan will be deducted from February's OTB.
- **Merchandise receipts** over plan will be deducted from February's OTB; receipts under plan will be added to February's OTB.

Depending on January's results and the resultant adjustments they have caused, you will undoubtedly either gain or lose OTB. If the change is dramatic, you may not be able to respond with corrections (adding, canceling, or delaying orders) to get back on plan for February, so you will have to implement any changes required as feasible in future months.

In my mind there are few retail disciplines, especially as your business grows, that can reap higher rewards than the OTB plan, except of course for the six-month plan, without which you cannot create the open-to-buy. To reiterate, the OTB builds the inventory for the more robust sales months and shrinks it for months with less planned sales—which should result in increased sales, less markdowns, and a greater turn—for greater profitability. It makes us control our business and focus on the inventory choices that must be made prudently. Otherwise, we can easily be like kids in a candy store who spend their whole week's allowance early in the week; and, because they have no money left, they must go without for the rest of the week. My only caution is that you must understand the OTB to use it appropriately; and you must also be aware that any significant deviations from plan can raise havoc with your OTB, which might take some time to work out before your flow of purchases should resume.

CHAPTER 15

Measuring Your Business with Three Key Ratios

Finally, in this short chapter I will discuss three ratios commonly used to measure the success of a retail business and to point to areas of opportunity:

- **Sales per Square Foot**
- **Turnover**
- **GMROI (gross margin return on inventory)**

After you calculate these performance ratios to measure areas needing improvement, you will want to compare them with the averages for your specific business because they vary a great deal among retail businesses and merchandise classifications. As with the many other statistics I have been discussing, to reiterate, the best sources to find the averages for your business are usually trade associations and trade publications. In addition, libraries and the web can often be productive for your type of business; and of course, if you can, get competitors' figures.

Sales per Square Foot

The Calculation. Sales per square foot is the easiest measure of the health and productivity of your business. It is also the most widely used of all the measurements, and since almost everyone figures it the same way, it allows you to easily compare your store against others. In addition to those sources previously mentioned, realtors and malls in your area may also be sources for this information.

To calculate your sales per square foot, divide your net annual sales by your *selling* square feet. (Do not include your stockroom, windows, cash wrap, etc., in this figure.)

Sales per Square Foot = Net Annual Sales ÷ Total Selling Square Feet

Example: Let us suppose Sally and Sam's store, which has annual net sales of $300,000, has 1,200 square feet of selling space.

$300,000 ÷ 1,200 = $250 sales per square foot.

For the simplest benchmark, many in retailing believe, if you are doing less than $200 per square foot, chances are your business is either overspaced or you are not selling enough from the space you have and should work to increase your productivity. But almost as important as your actual sales per square foot is planning and measuring improvement each year.

How to Improve Sales per Square Foot. The most obvious and effective way to improve your sales per square foot is to increase your sales through any number of the fundamental merchandising techniques that have been discussed throughout this book, like assortment selection and planning, pricing, and advertising. In addition, however, there are a couple of strategies directly related to the use of existing space that retailers often employ.

Getting more merchandise in the same footprint is the first option. You can do this by altering some store fixturing (like adding shelves to your display cabinets) or through store design modifications (like narrowing the aisles) in anticipation of increasing sales.

Shifting your space allocations is another way to increase your sales per square foot. Compare your various departments' sales per square foot to that of the total business, and over time shift your space allocations from the poorer-performing classifications to the better ones.

This strategy can be very effective, providing you do not lose sight of the need for a fully rounded assortment catering to your target customer, or you could be in danger of what some of us believe department stores have done over the years. For many years department stores have been increasing the amount of real estate for men's and ready-to-wear (the more profitable divisions) and decreasing the size of the home division (the least profitable) to the point where many home departments are either insignificant or don't exist anymore. This has resulted in alienating home furnishings customers and driving them to other types of retailers, risking the loss of those customers entirely.

Turnover

Inventory Turnover. This calculation measures how quickly you turn your stock and how well your inventory is performing, which has tremendous impact on your cash flow. The faster your turnover, the better your cash flow will be.

Although stock turns and turnover were discussed in the previous chapter in connection with six-month plans, turnover bears mentioning here as one of the major tools for judging the health of one's business. As was previously discussed, to figure turnover, divide your net sales (gross sales minus returns) by your average inventory at retail:

Turnover = Net Sales $ ÷ Average Inventory $

For example, Sally & Sam's had $300,000 net sales with an average inventory of $100,000, making for a 3 turn.

Some find it easier to think of stock turn in terms of weeks of supply rather than months of supply (as was previously discussed). Let's say you have a 2.5 turn. To get the weeks of supply, you divide fifty-two weeks by your stock turn. (52 ÷ 2.5 = 20.8 weeks of supply; 52 ÷ 2 = 26 weeks of supply 52 ÷ 3 = 17.3 weeks of supply). Or in months, a 2.5 turn is 4.8 months of supply (12 months ÷ 2.5); a 2 turn is six months; and a 3 turn is four months. As they say, "You *pays* your money, and you *takes* your choice," but the bottom line is this: the higher the turn, the better—provided you are not starving your inventory. This is worse than having too much inventory because having too little of the most-wanted goods will certainly drive your customers away and cost you sales.

You should research the average turn for your type of business because it varies a lot, but my experience has been that the absolute minimum healthy turn is at least 2, while most retail stores aim for 3 or higher and, as we have said, some retailer segments have very dramatically higher turns.

How Can You Improve Your Turnover? In addition to the various merchandise techniques to improve the desirability of your offering, there are a number of additional ways:

- **Adhere to your open-to-buy plan** when purchasing inventory, and begin to think of each purchase in terms of weeks/months of supply.
- **Replenish your best sellers** diligently to maximize them.
- **Place smaller orders** whenever it makes sense.
- **Take timely markdowns** to both prevent the buildup of slow-selling inventory, and allow for the purchasing of new items to refresh the assortment.
- **Expedite delivery from your suppliers,** and get new or wanted goods to the floor as quickly as possible.

Gross Margin Return on Inventory

GMROI. This measures your inventory productivity and how good an investment your business really is. This valuable tool can be used not only at the business level, but also at the department level, the category level, or even the SKU level, if you are so inclined.

This calculation can be done a couple of ways, but I think the simplest is measuring your return in dollars for every dollar invested using the following formula:

GMROI = Gross Margin $ ÷ Average Inventory at COST $

Remember, the formula for calculating **gross margin**:

Gross Margin $ = Sales $ – Cost of Goods Sold $

Next you'll need your average inventory at cost. To find your annual average use the twelve monthly ending inventories *at cost* plus the ending inventory from the previous year at cost and divide by thirteen. You must use cost because your investment in inventory was made at cost, even though you may think of it as retail for OTB purposes. To convert retail to cost, multiply by the reciprocal of your markup. For example, $1,000 retail times 60 percent (reciprocal of 40 percent markup) equates to $600 at cost.

Referring back to our earlier example for Sally and Sam's, which had annual sales of $300,000 and a cost of goods of $155,000, the gross margin was $145,000. The average inventory of $100,000 at retail when calculated at cost is $51,700 (the reciprocal of the gross margin of 48.3 percent). This means that every dollar invested in Sally and Sam's is returning $2.81 ($145,000 ÷ $51,700).

Since GMROI is an equation between gross margin and inventory, changing one or the other component can have a substantial impact. Also, I should point out that a slower-moving item or category at a higher gross margin can produce the same

GMROI as a faster-moving item or category at a lower gross margin. So, as you can see, in this instance there is more than one way to skin the cat!

Since, as was previously mentioned, the GMROI calculation can be done at the department level, or even the SKU level, it is a wonderful tool to determine which categories/items of inventory you may want to fund more than others, and which need some adjustment in either gross margin or inventory level to improve.

What Should Your GMROI Be? Like the other ratios we have mentioned, it varies tremendously based on what kind of operation you run and what your product line is. Articles by experts discussing GMROI across many industry lines claim it should be $1.50 to $2.00, while others writing about the retail business think $2.00 to $3.00 or even higher is more appropriate, depending again on the classification.

As I have already mentioned, many retail associations have figures on the various industries and their average GMROIs that can help you find the GMROI most typically associated with your business—so important because of the wide variance between retail segments. While this may be the best way, there are new sources every day, like the Retail Owners Institute's website I just found, which lists the average GMROI for each of fifty-two retail segments, as well as their gross margin and inventory turns, for free (http://retailowner.com/MembersOnly/GMROICalculator. aspx). For a monthly membership fee, the site also offers access to several calculators. This one lets you calculate your GMROI to compare to the most appropriate of the fifty-two categories they list.

While I cannot personally vouch for the veracity of all these numbers, I do believe a review of the categories will give you a good feel of retail GMROI (as well as gross margin percent and turnover) for various retail businesses. But even more than knowing the absolute numbers, the real value is in understanding how to use this tool (and the others) and in working toward constant improvement of your ratios to ultimately increase the profitability of your business.

So, there you have it—three important formulas to help you measure and improve your business and profitability to be added to the other methods we have already discussed, like gross margin and the all-important profit and loss statement.

This book has been dedicated to improving your profitability and success through learning the big guys' tricks of the trade. I hope you have found it of great value with its focus on how to determine which elements can be improved, as well as precisely how to improve them. The following few pages will review the considerable ground we have covered together.

Review & Conclusion

Since the purpose of this book is to help you, the independent shopkeeper, learn the tricks of the trade and level the playing field with the big guys, I have sought to impart the wisdom and insights gained in my over forty years' experience building successful retail businesses with them.

In the first couple of chapters, to set the stage, after assessing the state of the retail business today, for anyone considering entering retailing, *Be a Millionaire Shopkeeper* explores the various attributes of most successful independents I have known. While there are many traits, the most important are to be a competitive entrepreneur at heart, energetic, decisive, highly motivated, and a good multitasker, to name just a few. After I discuss what rewards the average independent shopkeeper might reap for his or her labor, the following chapters go on to discuss in detail what I believe are the most important tools, disciplines, and elements (except for luck) in creating a successful retail business and becoming a millionaire shopkeeper!

1. Developing Your Mission and Competitive Edge. Chapter 3 gets to the heart of it, the mission, which is the natural beginning and the cornerstone of your business. This chapter explains *how* to develop a clear, well-thought-out mission and how very important it is to your ultimate overall success. Your mission defines your store's reason for being, describes your purpose and niche in the marketplace, and states the focus of your business and its aims. I also stress that the stronger, more clearly differentiated, and more sustainable your competitive edge or USP is, the better your chances of long-range success.

2. Writing an Effective Business Plan. The next most critical element follows in chapter 4 with a discussion of the business plan, which is usually a necessity for funding, but also becomes the blueprint or road map to keep your business on course and serves as well as a major communication, motivational, and evaluation tool. I do believe that nothing succeeds like a plan, particularly in this case, and I outline several ways to get there and share important sources for help.

3. Conveying and Enhancing Your Mission with Five Important Factors. Chapter 5 explores the five most important factors: location; store design and ambience; pricing; customer service; and advertising—all with an end to maximizing their effectiveness for your mission and business. Since the first and key decision, the type of location you select, will profoundly influence the other four, the alternatives and factors to consider are discussed in detail. The balance of the chapter is devoted to the other factors and how you can make them work better for your mission and business. I discuss pricing strategies and methods, one of the most important keys to profitability, and their pros and cons. In the segments on store design/ambience and on customer service I review the basics, many of which are often not given their just due. Also covered are some special customer services that might enhance your USP and your strategic advantage. Finally, the stage is briefly set on conveying your mission through advertising for in-depth discussions that follow in chapters 11 and 12.

4. Shopping the Competition to Hone Your Competitive Advantage. The subject of chapter 6 is a methodology for reviewing your competition, including selecting which stores are *really* your competitors, and the chapter outlines how to search out the information that will lead to improving and strengthening your competitive edge.

5. Differentiating Your Product Line. For most retailers their product line is the key to success or failure, so this chapter (7) concentrates on exploring several ways to set it and your store apart. How to find trends and use them for differentiation (not so widely understood) is discussed at length, as is an area where the independent because of his smaller size has an advantage over the big guys, who cannot move as quickly. Other methods discussed and worth considering are finding and developing unique items as exclusives; utilizing different types of vendors (such as craftspeople, where once again you as an independent have the edge); creating your own gift sets; and developing private-label merchandise.

6. Utilizing Vendors More Effectively. In my opinion, this is the area perhaps least utilized by the independent shopkeeper. Properly used, suppliers can be your biggest partners in increasing your profits. In chapter 8 I discuss the different types of suppliers; how and where to find appropriate vendors; how to evaluate them; and most important of all, how to utilize them, including the concessions to seek for increasing profitability. Suppliers can indeed be where the gold is buried!

7. Refining Your Store and Product Line. Previously I have discussed how to differentiate your product line. In chapter 9 I take the discussion a step further and concentrate on how to make your products more wanted and salable. Your customers can be of invaluable assistance in helping you improve both your operation and your product line, and here is another instance when you have the upper hand over the big guys with one-to-one personal contact. There are also a number of key areas discussed that should be reviewed constantly to improve your product line; but perhaps the most enlightening is the process called the "style-out," which is covered in detail because it may be a new concept to many.

8. Maximizing a Trade Show or Buying Trip. While many buyers look at a buying trip or trade show as a good time, it is after all an investment in time and money, and there are a number of tricks that can make the experience far more fulfilling. In this chapter (10), I cover tips for preparing for the trip, ranging from making reservations and appointments; to making a shopping list and rough open-to-buy plan; and for efficiently shopping the show and the vendors to maximize the total experience.

9. Getting the Word Out. The first of the next two chapters (chapters 11 and 12) on advertising and communicating with your customers concentrates on growing your business through the traditional basics of advertising, sales promotion, and public relations. It defines, differentiates, and includes how to measure each of the three, as well as reveals sixteen tricks to make your advertising more effective; it also includes a myriad of often overlooked sales promotion opportunities with a checklist of in-store promotional events. Finally, tips for developing an effective PR campaign are included, and I discuss the worth of taglines/slogans and how to develop one for your shop.

10. Utilizing Internet Marketing. Nothing in modern times has revolutionized marketing more than the advent of the Internet. Online marketing cuts across the three major marketing disciplines discussed in the previous chapter and can work for any size or type of business. As well as the more traditional advertising tools, the Internet offers many new tools that I discuss at length (chapter 12) and help you access, use, and develop—such as websites, search engines, e-mail, blogs, and social media. With more than three-fourths of the US population on the Internet, virtually free and accessible from almost anywhere with a web-enabled device, it is a major opportunity to level the playing field with the big guys.

Its power and potential for building brands and customers cannot be ignored by the independent shopkeeper and must be embraced and developed.

11. Using the Profit and Loss Statement. In chapter 13 the profit and loss statement is defined and illustrated with a simple example. It is the most important financial document for your business, since it measures the success of your business; allows you to compare it to others; and helps you analyze areas that can be improved for added profitability, which I discuss at length with special emphasis on improving gross margin for greater profitability.

12. Merchandising Plans: The Six-Month Plan and the Open-to-Buy. These are the road maps and controls for your business, which properly conceived and executed are invaluable resources in running a profitable retail operation. Discussing these tools at great length in chapter 14, I take you through the thought process behind developing each of these, but I do recommend either purchasing good retail systems and/or getting help from someone who is very familiar with them (like a retail accountant) if you are not familiar with these tools. As for any plan, if they are ill-conceived they can do more harm than good. The six-month merchandise plan plans and tracks the essential elements of your business on a monthly basis: sales, stock levels, markdowns, and purchases; the open-to-buy budgets and controls your inventory purchases to facilitate having appropriate inventory levels to make your six-month merchandise plan.

13. Measuring Your Business with Three Key Ratios. Having discussed a number of tools to measure your business's profitability and analyze areas of opportunity, like the most important profit and loss statement, in the final chapter (15) I review three key ratios used for this purpose: sales per square foot, turnover, and GMROI (gross margin return on inventory). In addition, there are merchandise tips especially related to their specific improvement.

14. The Conclusion. As you know, I have tried to impart to you in this book the most important tricks that have contributed overwhelmingly to the growth and success of the best retailers. Now, armed with all this ammunition to help you compete effectively with them, it is time for me to wish you Godspeed in your quest to *Be a Millionaire Shopkeeper*.

CPSIA information can be obtained at www.ICGtesting.com
Printed in the USA
LVOW08s1030151215

466706LV00001B/293/P